LOS ANGELES REVIEW OF BOOKS

NO. 30 QUARTERLY JOURNAL

TRENDING

PUBLISHER: TOM LUTZ

EDITOR-IN-CHIEF: BORIS DRALYUK

MANAGING EDITOR: SONIA ALI

CONTRIBUTING EDITORS: SARA DAVIS, MASHINKA FIRUNTS HAKOPIAN, ELIZABETH METZGER, CALLIE SISKEL

ART DIRECTOR: PERWANA NAZIF

DESIGN DIRECTOR: LAUREN HEMMING

GRAPHIC DESIGNER: TOM COMITTA

ART CONTRIBUTORS: KAYLA EPHROS, ED MOCK, NARUMI NEK-PENEKPEN, BRONTEZ PURNELL, AND MONA VARICHON

PRODUCTION AND COPY DESK CHIEF: CORD BROOKS

EXECUTIVE DIRECTOR: IRENE YOON

MANAGING DIRECTOR: JESSICA KUBINEC

AD SALES: BILL HARPER

BOARD OF DIRECTORS: ALBERT LITEWKA (CHAIR), JODY ARMOUR, REZA ASLAN, BILL BENENSON, LEO BRAUDY, EILEEN CHENG-YIN CHOW, MATT GALSOR, ANNE GERMANACOS, TAMERLIN GODLEY, SETH GREENLAND, GERARD GUILLEMOT, DARRYL HOLTER, STEVEN LAVINE, ERIC LAX, TOM LUTZ, SUSAN MORSE, SHARON NAZARIAN MARY SWEENEY, LYNNE THOMPSON, BARBARA VORON, MATTHEW WEINER, JON WIENER, JAMIE WOLF

COVER ART: KAYLA EPHROS, DESIGNER GOD (PEACE OF MIND), 2021 OIL PASTEL ON PAPER, 17 X 12.5 INCHES. COURTESY OF THE ARTIST AND IN LIEU.

INTERNS & VOLUNTEERS: THOMAS WEE, EMILY SMIBERT

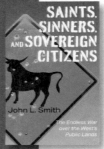

"A pure erotic fury. An unapologetic delight."

—Lidia Yuknavitch, bestselling author of _Verge_ and _The Book of Joan_

Literary short fiction from all-star contributors exploring love and desire, BDSM, and interests across the sexual spectrum that's

"Groundbreaking."
—O, The Oprah Magazine

"Provocative, poignant, and sublimely written."
—Town & Country

"Arresting."
—The New Yorker

Roxane Gay Kim Fu
Callum Angus Vanessa Clark
Melissa Febos Alexander Chee
Zeyn Joukhadar Brandon Taylor
Chris Kraus Peter Mountford
Larissa Pham Cara Hoffman
Carmen Maria Machado

Kink

STORIES

NATIONAL BESTSELLER

Edited by
R.O. Kwon and
Garth Greenwell

CONTENTS

NO. 30 QUARTERLY JOURNAL:
TRENDING

PRINCETON UNIVERSITY PRESS

"Bechky's portrait of the daily conflict faced by crime lab workers should prove enlightening to outsiders. . . . This account of a fascinating work world manages to be both scholarly and engaging."

—Kathy Reichs, *New York Times Book Review*

"This essay collection assesses the stakes and real-world relevance of Nabokov's writing, from his lectures and short stories to his major novels. It's a great read if you're a Nabokov fan, or if you've ever wondered, 'Why did this guy write Lolita?'"

—*Literary Hub*

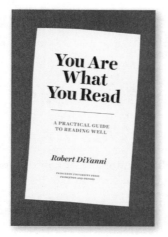

"Simply a joy. . . . DiYanni provides practical strategies that guide readers to a sustained, significant appreciation of literary works."

—Linda Costanzo Cahir, Kean University

"A selection of charming prose pieces from the early years of the legendary movie director and screenwriter."

—Christian Rogowski, Amherst College

LETTER FROM THE EDITORS

Dear reader,

After a year and some change spent indoors and glued to screens of all sizes, we have watched a lot of the same things — some with horror, some for laughs, and some for distraction. Often these sights and sounds have bonded us as families and friends, and occasionally they have motivated us to act as collective forces. From the mother and daughter renegotiating their relationship in Natalia Reyes's story "The Wash" to the Egyptian feminists of the roaring 1920s chronicled in Raphael Cormack's "Doing Justice to Egyptian Feminists" the pieces in this issue dramatize reckonings with identity in relation to others and to the spirit of a given era. Stephen Marche's "The Thing on the Phone," for instance, forces us to question the degree to which our stories are our own, as opposed to products of ever-advancing technology. Natasha Rao, on the other hand, finds the promise of renewal in dark times, writing, "I fling wide the door to feel / which way the wind is moving, / barely open my mouth before / a new species of bird evolves / and fills the air / with uncountable versions / of the freshest song."

We hope these essays, stories, and poems offer an expansive view of where our global culture is tending and trending.

— Boris Dralyuk, Editor-in-Chief,
   and Sonia Ali, Managing Editor

Thanks so much to the following people who generously donated to our 2020 Matching Grant Fund Drive in support of this print edition:

Philip Alcabes, Kelly Anderson, Jon Robin Baitz, Glen Brunman, Greyson Bryan, Ranita Chatterjee, Michael Coffey, Jonathan Cohn, Loraine Despres Eastlake, Steve Diskin, Victoria and Saul Faerstein, Stephen Fishbach, Dede Gardner, David Kaye, Larry Lasker and Anita Keys, David Levinson, Mary Helen McMurran, Christie Morehead, Michael Motia, Michael Nava, Virginia Newmyer, Valerie Polichar, Lelia Scheu, Peter Sherwood, David St. John and Anna Journey, Florian Suter, Jaak Treiman, Liz Walters, Maria and Kenneth Warren, John Webber, and Mitchell Wilson.

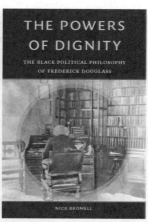

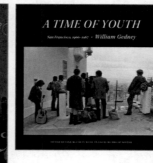

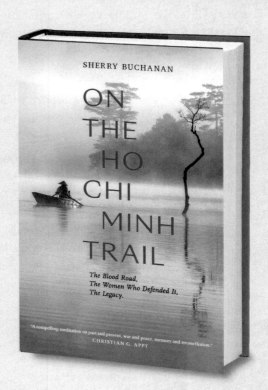

BIZARRE-PRIVILEGED ITEMS
IN THE UNIVERSE:
THE LOGIC OF LIKENESS
by Paul North

"At once free and rigorous, impertinent and lucid...a philosophical tour de force."
—GEORGES DIDI-HUBERMAN

ABSENTEES:
ON VARIOUSLY MISSING PERSONS
by Daniel Heller-Roazen

"Weaves scholarly rigor together with theoretical vision...Heller-Roazen is operating at the height of his powers."
—BERNADETTE MEYLER

NEW IN PAPERBACK
HISTORICAL GRAMMAR
OF THE VISUAL ARTS
by Aloïs Riegl

"A crucial precedent for the current reevaluation of the theory and practice of art history today." —BENJAMIN BINSTOCK

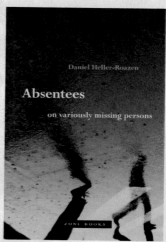

SPRING 2021

ZONE BOOKS

DISTRIBUTED BY PRINCETON UNIVERSITY PRESS I ZONEBOOKS.ORG

Kayla Ephros, *and today (10/105)*, 2021, Oil pastel on paper, 13 x 11 inches.
Courtesy of the artist and in lieu.

SHADOWS WALKING: WITH WALLACE STEVENS IN NEW HAVEN

LANGDON HAMMER

For Susan Howe

In the metaphysical streets
of the physical town

"In the metaphysical streets, the profoundest forms / Go with the walker subtly walking there." This is Stevens in canto XI of "An Ordinary Evening in New Haven." Walking in this long poem is a vehicle for meditation and a trope for the writing of poetry. The figure works the other way around too: writing poetry is like walking in a city. In the case of New Haven, as Stevens said in a letter, a walk brings you into contact not with "grim reality but plain reality," "plain" meaning daily and ordinary, physical and visible, apparent. The world as it is.

Beyond and behind apparent reality are Alpha and Omega, ultimate things and "profoundest forms." New Haven was founded in 1638 by Puritans from the Massachusetts Bay Colony who desired to build a theocratic community, based in Mosaic Law. More than three centuries later, Stevens's poem broods on the Puritan foundations of the city. History for the Puritans moved toward apocalypse and the ultimate reality of New Jerusalem. Stevens rejects the idea: "Reality is the beginning not the end, / Naked Alpha, not the hierophant Omega."

The Quinnipiac River flows south into New Haven Harbor and Long Island Sound. In Hamden, just north of New Haven, it passes Hobbomock, the Stone Giant, a rock formation honored by the Quinnipiac, who called themselves "the original people." "Quinnipiac" is an English form of another name meaning "place of the long water." "Dawnland" was their name for the mountains, woods, and marshes they inhabited in present-day New England. Their treaty with the English settlers of New Haven made them possibly the first indigenous North Americans confined to a reservation.

The first planned city in North America, New Haven was laid out in a grid of nine blocks. The central block was the Green. Puritan city planners designed the area sufficient to accommodate the assembly of souls they expected to be saved at the Second Coming of Christ. The Green had a prison, church, school, cemetery, market, and grazing cows. When the capital of Connecticut was shared between Hartford and New Haven, the statehouse stood on the Green.

The Mende people of the Amistad rebellion were imprisoned in New Haven from September 1839 to August 1840 while their case was tried in District and Circuit courts. Local citizens paid a "New York shilling" each to see the Africans in the Church Street jail where they were held in a cage built for them. Periodically the captives were brought out on the Green for exercise. Today a statue of their leader, Joseph Cinqué, stands on the site of the jail in front of City Hall.

"An Ordinary Evening in New Haven" is composed of 31 cantos, each of which consists of six three-line stanzas of unrhymed pentameter. The pattern meant nothing in particular to Stevens. To Norman Holmes Pearson, a Yale English professor, he wrote: "The essential thing in form is to be free in whatever form is used. A free form does not assure freedom. As a form it is just one more form. So that it comes to this, I suppose, that I believe in freedom regardless of form."

In the 1960s, with a cane and a leg brace we bought at Yale Surgical after her second stroke, but still able to take the bus downtown, scraping her black shoe as she walked, my grandmother, who was born and lived her whole life in New Haven, spent her days sitting on a bench on the Church Street side of the Green, watching people and gossiping with other old women. For my grandmother, my mother would say, "The New Haven Green is the center of the universe."

¤

In 1979, I was a senior Yale English major living a mile from the campus. Out on the sunny bland avenue, I watched Harold Bloom punctually on Tuesdays walk to teach his class. He advanced a little tilted to one side, his shoulders sloping back, his eyes half-closed, and his mouth moving, without sound. His feet seemed to glide along rather than take steps. The effect was of a sort of ship. He seemed to be at

CULTURAL HISTORIES & LITERATURES
From Ancient Greece to Modern Los Angeles

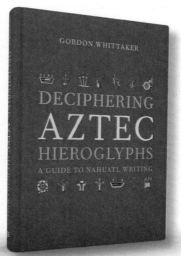

"The fascinating world of Aztec glyphic writing, magnificently explained by an erudite expert in the ancient art of tlacuilolli."

—**María Castañeda De La Paz,**
Universidad Nacional Autónoma de México

"With insight and wit, Robert C. Ritchie traces the long fascination with beaches."

—**Alan Taylor, author of**
Thomas Jefferson's Education

"A much needed, must-read book on Asian Pacific Americans and how we too have sung America."

—**Karen L. Ishizuka, Chief Curator,**
Japanese American National Museum

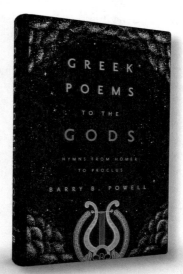

"Powell puts his great translation skills to work, bringing out the texts' epic tone, piety, and humor."

—**Carolina López-Ruiz,**
The Ohio State University

"Taylor, a master of historical writing on colonial Mexico, shows Spanish rule failing and flourishing at the same time."

—**Davíd Carrasco,**
Harvard Divinity School

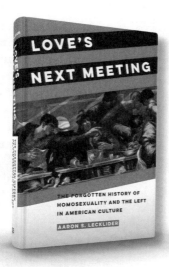

"Engrossing, beautifully written, and wryly humorous from beginning to end."

—**Mary Helen Washington, author of**
The Other Blacklist

UNIVERSITY of CALIFORNIA PRESS

www.ucpress.edu

once in the world — on foot, on schedule — and somewhere high and far away.

Stevens walked to his office at the Hartford Accident and Indemnity Company. In his oral biography of Stevens, from 1977, Peter Brazeau quotes Florence Berkman:

> Every morning, like clockwork, he used to walk down Terry Road about nine o'clock, just about the time I was standing by my kitchen sink. I'd always get a thrill. In the afternoon, he'd walk back, this very slow stride of his. Usually, if it was summer or good weather, I'd be outdoors with some of the neighbors' children. I'd make them stop and look at him, and I'd say, "I want you to remember this is a great poet."

Bloom published *Wallace Stevens: The Poems of Our Climate* in 1977. The epigraph is from Stevens's "From the Packet of Anacharsis": "and Bloom with his vast accumulation / Stands and regards and repeats the primitive lines." "Bloom" is an invented character, not Harold Bloom. Harold knew that of course. But he must have felt that, on some level, Stevens was writing about him, to him. He wanted to hear Stevens say his name.

When I was Bloom's student in 1981, I worked so hard on my papers it was difficult to finish them. I dropped out of school and took a job as a copyeditor, until I was fired for the mess I made of a military history manuscript (topic: American munitions during World War II). Five days a week at 7:00 a.m., I lay on a psychoanalyst's couch. Often I said nothing, or almost nothing.

Two weeks before he died, I visited Harold and Jeanne on Linden Street. Harold was strapped into a wheelchair. A nurse, the young Black woman who had let me in, sat reading in the next room, so quietly you could forget she was there. Harold's face, always mobile and expressive, seemed clarified: a skull coming forward. As usual, copies of his recent books were stacked on the dining table. He took two and inscribed them for me, in his shaking hand, "with love." But he never read those papers on "Resolution and Independence" and "A Child Is Being Beaten."

¤

By the time I became a Yale professor in 1987, Bloom visited the English Department offices only occasionally to collect his mail, accompanied by a student or assistant. There were rumors about his relationship with X, or with Y. He was very heavy at this point, and he liked to wear a baggy leather bomber jacket. One day, in the mail room, he saw me in a suit and said with surprising sharpness, "My dear, you look like you work in a bank."

Across from the English Department on High Street stands Skull and Bones, one of the "secret" societies that enroll select Yale seniors — private clubs with their own property, endowments, and lore. The story goes that members of Skull and Bones broke into the grave of Geronimo, in 1918, and brought the warrior's skull back to the society, where, according to one report, they exhibited it "together with his well-worn femurs, bit and saddle horn."

Prescott Bush led the party of grave robbers, supposedly. Bush became a

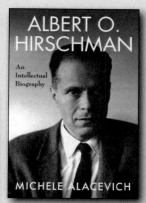
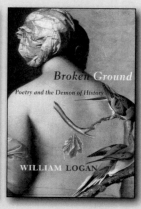

powerful banker and a United States senator from Connecticut. His son George served as director of the CIA, vice president, and the 41st president of the United States. George's son George served for two terms as the 43rd president. The Bushes — three generations of Bonesmen.

I've walked past that crypt-like building, the color of dried blood, for more than 40 years, on my way to lunch or class. Usually I don't notice it.

¤

Stevens composed poetry while walking. Getting his body going must have helped him get his words flowing, a cadence coordinated with a stride. He reacted to his surroundings even as he remained at a remove, arranging phrases in his mind. Comma, clause, enjambment — one leg swings past the other, crossing the avenue.

Richard Sunbury, a mail boy in the office, remembers lunch-hour walks with Stevens: "He most always had some envelopes stuffed in his pockets, and he'd just pull them out and write on the back." Then Stevens would give what he'd written to his secretary, Mrs. Baldwin, and ask her, "Would you run a transcript of this?" She returned with a typed sheet, saying, "I don't know what this is all about, but here it is." "She was an older woman," Sunbury recalls, "and she was a humdinger."

Stevens is a difficult poet, an intellectual poet, whose work broods on itself as it hovers above the real. The author of *Wallace Stevens: The Poems of Our Climate* is a difficult critic. There is a sense of Bloom competing with Stevens for the power that comes with the metaphysical view.

In seminar, Bloom didn't lecture. He asked questions — often the same question, over and over. Sometimes he wanted

to know what source was being echoed in a text. Comically, hands would go up and students would try out Bloomian favorites — Shelley, Emerson, Nietzsche? But more often what he was doing was not a guessing game. He was inviting us to join him in his reading of a text, to interrogate it with him, muse on it, and simply stay with it longer than we had thought possible.

There were no answers because he was reading for something that wasn't there: what the text was silent about. Bloom says in his Stevens book: "A poem begins because there is an absence." "Surface reading" and "distant reading" are fashionable techniques among literature professors today. Those were not Bloom's method. But neither was it "close reading." He was interested in white space, the fugitive, the repressed. John Hollander said to me once: "As a reader, Bloom has X-ray vision. He doesn't notice the red coat you're wearing, but he can see where your leg is broken."

¤

Stevens's "Professor Eucalyptus of New Haven" seeks divinity "[i]n New Haven with an eye that does not look // Beyond the object." The clumsy repetition of the city's name makes fun of the literalism that fetishizes the words on a page. Close readers are too concerned with the verbal icon or well-wrought urn, text as object rather than occasion. They repeat what has already been said.

Eucalyptus: from the Greek, meaning "well covered." Apocalypse is an "uncovering." In this anti-apocalyptic poem, shadows and shadings are a good thing. Doublings and disguise. Spies have "cover lives." An ordinary job allows them

Faithful

Our 606 Universal Shelving System
was designed by Dieter Rams 60
years ago to help you live better,
with less, that lasts longer.
Start small. Add to it. Rearrange it.

Contact your dependable Vitsœ
planner via our website.

to do their real work in secret. The same may be true of poets. Think of T. S. Eliot, the banker, or Wallace Stevens, the insurance man. (See Hollander, *Reflections on Espionage*, 1976.)

Stevens was uncomfortable in academic settings, formal and informal. One evening he got drunk among a group of Harvard English professors. He tried to amuse them with "smoking-car stories," until Walter Jackson Bate, biographer of Samuel Johnson and John Keats, stopped him with a scowl. "I'm afraid I'm not amusing you, Mr. Bate," Stevens said. Bate barked: "You'll have to be a lot funnier than that to make me laugh, Stevens!" Stevens turned red, and stopped talking.

He had an easier relationship with F. O. Matthiessen, Harvard's great Americanist. They had dinner on occasion, and exchanged cordial letters, including one in which Stevens carefully explained his cryptic Florida-funeral-parlor poem, "The Emperor of Ice-Cream."

Shadowed by the atomic bomb and a Cold War waged via arcane spy-craft, proxy conflicts, and domestic surveillance, the late 1940s were in some ways even darker and more threatening than the war years had been. Apocalypse is a motif throughout *The Auroras of Autumn* (1950), the book in which "An Ordinary Evening in New Haven" was collected. In 1947, Matthiessen wrote:

> All of Stevens' later work has been written against the realization that we live in a time of violent disorder. The most profound challenge in his poems is his confidence that even in such a time, even on the verge of ruin, a man can recreate afresh his world out of the unfailing utilization of his inner resources.

Three years later Matthiessen fell to his death from a 12th-floor room in a Boston hotel.

The Harvard Crimson quoted the note Matthiessen left indicating his wishes for burial and his state of mind at the time of his suicide: "I am depressed over world conditions. I am a Christian and a Socialist." "The evil thing, for him," Stevens wrote to Norman Holmes Pearson, "was that he was a man of ideas who found himself being crawled over by a lot of people from a quite different sort of world. [...] I was struck by the fact that he desired to be buried near his mother at Springfield, like a man left alone and intensely hurt by it." Stevens knew that Matthiessen was being investigated by McCarthy's House Un-American Activities Committee, and that he was mourning for his companion of 20 years, Russell Cheney, who had died in 1945.

Cheney and Matthiessen, the younger man in the couple, graduated from Yale a generation apart. Their relationship was an open secret. Both men were members of Skull and Bones. When he climbed out of the hotel window, Matthiessen left his society key in the room.

¤

Stevens spoke at Yale for the first time in 1948, at the age of 69, when Louis Martz, an English professor, invited him to lecture. Before the event, Stevens opened his briefcase and showed Martz how it was organized, with business documents on one side and poetry on the other. He read his essay "Effects of Analogy" and the poem "A Primitive Like an Orb." He spoke in a voice so low no one could hear

New and Noteworthy

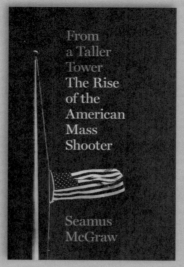

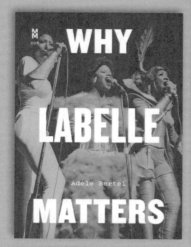

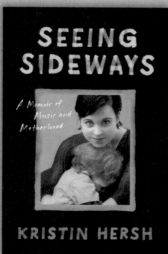

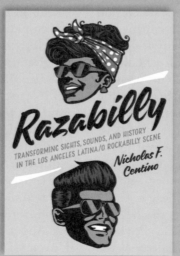

Why Labelle Matters
BY ADELE BERTEI

Crafting a legacy all their own, the reinvented Labelle subverted the "girl group" aesthetic to invoke the act's Afrofuturist spirit and make manifest their vision of Black womanhood.

$18.95 | PAPERBACK

Seeing Sideways
A Memoir of Music and Motherhood
BY KRISTIN HERSH

A follow-up to the critically acclaimed *Rat Girl*, this beautifully written memoir takes readers on an emotional journey through the author's life as she reflects on thirty years of music and motherhood.

$27.95 | HARDCOVER

From a Taller Tower
The Rise of the American Mass Shooter
BY SEAMUS McGRAW

There is no silence on earth deeper than the silence between gunshots; *From a Taller Tower* faces the depths of that silence, which follows in the wake of the mass shootings that have plagued the United States.

$27.95 | HARDCOVER

Far from Respectable
Dave Hickey and His Art
BY DANIEL OPPENHEIMER

The first book on the critic and essayist Dave Hickey, *Far from Respectable* examines the life and work of this controversial figure, whose writing changed the discourse around art and popular culture.

$24.95 | HARDCOVER

Razabilly
Transforming Sights, Sounds, and History in the Los Angeles Latina/o Rockabilly Scene
BY NICHOLAS F. CENTINO

An engrossing deep dive into the sights, sounds, and sensibilities of the Latina/o Rockabilly scene in Los Angeles, its ties to working-class communities, and its dissemination through the post-NAFTA global landscape.

$29.95 | PAPERBACK

him past the third row. When someone asked him to speak up, he agreed, then lowered his voice further.

A faculty dinner followed at Pearson's home. After it, Stevens worried that he had insulted Cleanth Brooks and his wife, Tinkum. Brooks was mystified when Stevens apologized to him a full year later. "I really was completely shocked and surprised," Brooks said. "We had had a very pleasant conversation." He thought Stevens a "true poet" because he let "his imagination oftentimes completely alter his picture of what a situation was."

Pearson, a Yale graduate, came from a family that had settled in Massachusetts in 1639. He and his wife Susan lived on Goodrich Street in a Tudor-style house with a slate roof and casement windows built for the Winchester family in 1928. Susan Silliman Bennett's ancestors included a line of Yale scientists on one side and the founder and subsequent presidents of Winchester Repeating Arms on the other.

The maker of "The Gun that Won the West," Winchester began manufacturing in New Haven in 1871. The company was the largest employer in the city for much of the 20th century. As a high school student during World War II, my mother had a job on the assembly line, turning out the M1 Garand rifle, standard issue for American GIs.

Pearson served during the war in the OSS in London, then helped to organize the Central Intelligence Agency with his former student and OSS colleague James Jesus Angleton, who became the head of American counterintelligence. Pearson's code name was "Puritan." Angleton was a Yale English major and a Bonesman.

During the Second Great Migration, Black families from the American South moved to New Haven and took jobs in the Winchester factory as production expanded to meet the wartime demand. Winchester's fortunes declined after the war, and the Irish, Poles, and Italians, who had held factory jobs for the first half of the century, moved to nearby towns, while redlining confined Black residents to the neighborhood around the factory.

New Haven's guns had won not only the West but two World Wars. By the 1970s, guns were common on New Haven streets. One evening I opened the door of my graduate-student apartment, and the officer at the bottom of the stairs turned and pointed his pistol at me, his arms locked, as on TV. I put my hands against the wall and spread my legs. He relaxed a little when he saw we both were white.

The conditions that made guns part of daily life in the city have improved, but only so much. In 2017, the so-called Goodrich Street Boys, seven men who grew up in the shadow of a factory that once employed 20,000 people, were arrested for a rash of shootings in turf wars with rival gangs. In the same neighborhood, in 2019, Hamden and Yale police fired 16 times at a Black couple who were sitting in a parked car, unarmed. The university employs its own police force, consisting of 93 officers and detectives. So far this year six people have been shot to death in New Haven.

Pearson's home is currently advertised as a pre-foreclosure sale. Under "What I Love About This Home," the realtor says: "Postwar CIA founded here."

¤   ¤

ASSOCIATION FOR **JEWISH STUDIES**

Congratulations to the 2021 Jordan Schnitzer Book Award Winners

Presented by the Association for Jewish Studies

WINNERS

BIBLICAL STUDIES, RABBINICS, AND JEWISH HISTORY & CULTURE IN ANTIQUITY

Time in the Babylonian Talmud: Natural and Imagined Times in Jewish Law and Narrative

Cambridge University Press
LYNN KAYE, Brandeis University

JEWS AND THE ARTS: MUSIC, PERFORMANCE, AND VISUAL

Writing on the Wall: Graffiti and the Forgotten Jews of Antiquity

Princeton University Press
KAREN B. STERN, Brooklyn College

MODERN JEWISH HISTORY AND CULTURE: EUROPE AND ISRAEL

Prince of the Press: How One Collector Built History's Most Enduring and Remarkable Jewish Library

Yale University Press
JOSHUA TEPLITSKY, Stony Brook University

SOCIAL SCIENCE, ANTHROPOLOGY, AND FOLKLORE

The Jews' Indian: Colonialism, Pluralism, and Belonging in America

Rutgers University Press
DAVID S. KOFFMAN, York University

FINALISTS

BIBLICAL STUDIES, RABBINICS, AND JEWISH HISTORY & CULTURE IN ANTIQUITY

Job: A New Translation

Yale University Press
EDWARD L. GREENSTEIN, Bar-Ilan University

JEWS AND THE ARTS: MUSIC, PERFORMANCE, AND VISUAL

Possessed Voices: Aural Remains from Modernist Hebrew Theater

SUNY Press
RUTHIE ABELIOVICH, University of Haifa

MODERN JEWISH HISTORY AND CULTURE: EUROPE AND ISRAEL

The Rise of the Modern Yiddish Theater

Indiana University Press
ALYSSA QUINT, YIVO

SOCIAL SCIENCE, ANTHROPOLOGY, AND FOLKLORE

Fighting for Dignity: Migrant Lives at Israel's Margins

University of Pennsylvania Press
SARAH S. WILLEN, University of Connecticut

The Association for Jewish Studies is the largest learned society and professional organization representing Jewish Studies scholars worldwide. Visit **associationforjewishstudies.org** to learn more about our work and the upcoming 2021 Jordan Schnitzer Book Award competition.

Watch interviews with the winners at
asociationforjewishstudies.org/awards2020

This book award program has been made possible by generous funding from Jordan Schnitzer and Arlene Schnitzer through the Harold & Arlene Schnitzer Family Fund of the Oregon Jewish Community Foundation.

Spooks. Ghosts. The word entered American English from the Dutch in the 18th century. In the 1940s, it became a slang term for spies. Around the same time, "spooks" became, for whites, a slur for Black people — because they were shadowy, hard to see. Hard for white people to see.

Rickey Laurentiis's poem "Of the Leaves that Have Fallen," published in 2014, is a passionate reply to Stevens's "Like Decorations [...]." Laurentiis answers Stevens's 50-part poem with 50 meditations on the Black victims of American lynching — a "grim reality" that Stevens, with the N-word there in his title, calls to mind and then (brutally, haughtily?) ignores. Laurentiis says:

> To negotiate the dark you must
>   open, you must open
> To the dark: dirt, the hundred
>   worms beneath you, beneath
> Where hands come to claw the
>   dirt, let, and lay you down.

Stevens asks: "Can all men, together, avenge / One of the leaves that have fallen in autumn?" No, he decides, "the wise man avenges by building his city in snow."

When I was a child, my grandmother had snow-white hair, neatly brushed, and so soft-seeming I wanted to pet it. To Gammie, Black people were "the coloreds." The word was gravelly in her mouth, as if she were trying to swallow something, or spit it out. Whereas when my mother mentioned Mary, "a colored girl," her childhood friend, the word was tender. Beside it, "white" meant blank and cold.

"No one living a snowed-in life / can sleep without a blindfold," Terrance Hayes says in "Snow for Wallace Stevens." Stevens is Hayes's "foe, / the clean-shaven, gray-suited, gray patron / of Hartford, the emperor of whiteness / blue as a body made of snow."

¤

In 2019, someone posted Hayes's "Snow for Wallace Stevens" in response to a tweet by Saeed Jones deploring Stevens's racism. Others posted Laurentiis's "Of the Leaves that Have Fallen" and Major Jackson's prose comment "Wallace Stevens After 'Lunch.'" Jones and Jackson were both reacting to a story in Joan Richardson's biography of Stevens.

Stevens was a judge for the National Book Award in poetry in 1952. All six judges were white men. While they waited for one of the judges who had been delayed "by a snowstorm," the rest looked at photos of the judges from the previous year. These included Gwendolyn Brooks, who had served on the jury when Stevens won the prize for *The Auroras of Autumn*. When he saw the photo of Brooks, Richardson writes,

> Stevens remarked, "Who's the coon?" (The meeting, it should be noted, took place after lunch, which for the poet had probably begun with two healthy martinis and continued with a fine bottle of wine.) Noticing the reaction of the group to his question, he asked, "I know you don't like to hear people call a lady a coon, but who is it?"

In the stream of replies to Jones's tweet, the playwright Paula Vogel wrote: "Thanks for gluing history to Wallace

GIACOMO DONIS

THE EMPTY SHIELD
A DECISION
POLITICAL AUTOBIOGRAPHY

Available on **Amazon**
and **SPDBooks.org**

A people's history and the horror of war:
Howard Zinn meets *Apocalypse Now*. Political
autobiography. March 1972, about to graduate
from NYU. A journey: two days and nights in the
New York subway. Love it or leave it. A decision:
become a Great Academic Marxist; blow up the
Williamsburg Bridge; go into exile. Vietnam
Veterans with placards, for and against the war.
Seven placard-men at the seven gates of Thebes,
brandishing their shields.

A decision. Political or personal? Or pure Zen?
Mind or no-mind? Kill for peace! Dylan, Hendrix,
or the Fugs. The two Suzukis, or Dogen. Monk
and Coltrane! The relation between Hegel's logic
of thinking as such and his logic of practice, which
does not exist. The *screech* of the subway stops.
A fork where three roads cross, the realm of
shadows, what is to be done? A Chinese menu?
Stab it! Stab it with your fork!

But what I, myself, decide is not the point. The
point is the question of 'what a decision is and
what making a decision means.' The answer is
'never stop asking.' Ask yourself. Ask FDR, JFK,
LBJ, or a Vietnam War veteran of your choice. Ask
Nixon, Kissinger—Trump! Never mind Trump! Biden
just 'decided' to unite the country! A decision.
Foe is friend! Ye great decision-makers, have you
ever asked yourselves *what a decision is and what
making a decision means!* That is the question.
The Empty Shield asks it. Repeatedly, repetitiously,
abysally, and, possibly, once and for all.

978-1-912477-92-0 • Paperback $21.99
482 Pages • Political Autobiography
WWW.EYEWEARPUBLISHING.COM

Stevens. Never knew it; now I can save time and not read him."

Hayes's collection of poems *Lighthead* won the National Book Award in 2010. In "Snow for Wallace Stevens," included in that book, he asks,

> Who is not more than his
> limitations?
> Who is not the blood in a wine
> barrel
> and the wine as well? I too, hav-
> ing lost faith
> in language, have placed my faith
> in language.
> Thus, I have a capacity for love
> without forgiveness.

¤

The subject of "A Primitive Like an Orb," the poem Stevens read at Yale in 1948, is "the central poem," "the poem of the whole." By "primitive," Stevens means primary, original, essential. He is using "primitive" as a noun, personifying the "poem" as if it were a man native to the place, made out of the place. By the end of the poem, the figure grows into "a giant on the horizon." Stevens must have been thinking of Sleeping Giant, the mountain sacred to the Quinnipiac, which he would have seen from the train whenever he passed between Hartford and New Haven.

Stevens speaks of "the central poem" as a "huge, high harmony." We come upon it "a little," and then "suddenly," in the form of "lesser poems," by which he means actual poems and art works as well as casual perceptions and intimations, stray thoughts and observations, in the course of daily life — where your mind goes when you walk about. These "lesser poems" are parts of the whole, a grand orchestration that they together compose, and that yet exceeds them: reality in its fullness.

Which must remain virtual, always beyond or behind us, because it is a thing "apart," known only "[b]y means of a separate sense." Ultimate reality is ever in motion: "It is and it / Is not and, therefore, is." That "therefore," insisting on logical proof in a grammar that defies it, is a nice touch. Stevens is parodying, but also appropriating for poetry, the expository prose of the professors in his audience in New Haven.

The poem of the whole: Does it include a Tudor house on Goodrich Street? The manufacture of firearms? My mother and Mary? F. O. Matthiessen, motionless on the sidewalk? What about Mrs. Baldwin, the humdinger? Who typed the copy of "A Primitive Like an Orb" Stevens read in New Haven? Not everyone has a name. Gets a name.

¤

After hosting him in 1948, Pearson encouraged Stevens to give papers on poetics. Stevens did, but he doubted the results. He thought his essays were a "compost pile and should therefore properly be kept out on the back lot. But what has determined this is the idea that my real job is poetry and not papers about poetry, so far as I have any real job."

In 1949, the Connecticut Academy of Arts and Sciences invited Stevens to read a poem for the Academy's sesquicentennial. He composed "An Ordinary Evening in New Haven" for this event, which included on the program a paper by the biophysicist Max Delbrück and a concerto for trumpet and bassoon by Paul Hindemith.

About his plans for the poem, Stevens

commented: "I wanted to have something that would relate to the occasion but not directly. So I just fixed on this idea of a poem about a walk in New Haven, but then branching out." This procedure was typical of him. "I start with a concrete thing, and it tends to become so generalized that it isn't any longer a local place." Before the event, he read the poem to his wife, "as is my custom." When he had finished, Mrs. Stevens put her hands over her eyes, and said, "They're not going to understand this."

"The real is only the base," Stevens says in his notebook. Then he adds: "But it is the base."

The cityscape of New Haven is generalized in "An Ordinary Evening." Houses are "transparent dwellings" in "an impalpable town." When Stevens refers to the Yale campus and the churches on the Green as "such chapels and such schools," "such" keeps them generic. "A glassy ocean lying at the door" is Long Island Sound and the "sea of glass" in Revelation. The city is bounded by East Rock on one side and West Rock on the other — cliff formations similar to Sleeping Giant that were created by the retreat of the continental ice shelf about 20,000 years ago. Stevens refers to these mountains as "the rock of autumn, glittering, / Ponderable source of each imponderable."

Evening, the time of day in Stevens's poem, is relevant: a time of transition, of doubleness and ambiguity. "If, then, New Haven is half sun, what remains, // At evening, after dark, is the other half," city of shades and shadows, where particulars are smudged and blurred, and meanings are "less legible."

¤

In 1942, Stevens had this exchange with a young man from New Haven who had come to visit him in Hartford:

I often get away to New Haven for a weekend — find it a good place to relax, entertain myself.

You mean you actually find New Haven a relief from Hartford?

Why, yes.

Strange. That is just the way I feel about Hartford.

There! That shows how silly it is, really. A state of mind.

On those weekend getaways, Stevens probably stayed in the Taft on the corner of College and Chapel streets, a splendid hotel close to bars, restaurants, the Shubert Theatre, and Yale's Old Campus. In canto IX of "An Ordinary Evening," he writes:

We keep coming back and com-
    ing back
To the real: to the hotel instead of
    the hymns
That fall upon it out of the wind.

Those "hymns" are part of "the huge, high harmony" in "A Primitive Like an Orb." They are also church hymns, like the Anglican "Holy, Holy, Holy":

Holy, Holy, Holy! All the saints
    adore Thee,
Casting down their golden
    crowns around the glassy sea;
Cherubim and seraphim falling
    down before Thee,
Which wert, and art, and

evermore shalt be.

"It is and is / Not and, therefore, is" revises "Which wert, and art, and evermore shall be." An ongoing present, without past or future.

¤

In canto XV, Stevens asserts: "The instinct for heaven had its counterpart" in "[t]he instinct for earth, for New Haven, for his room, / The gay tournamonde as of a single world // In which he is and as and is are one." The "he" is Professor Eucalyptus, but it could be anyone meditating on the earthly as manifest in a place like New Haven. When his editor questioned the neologism "tournamonde," Stevens defended it: "For me it creates an image of a world in which things revolve and the word is therefore appropriate in the collocation of is and as."

You walk the same streets year after year. Sometimes things change so slowly they seem not to change at all. But they do. So-and-So lived there, Mrs. Pappadopoulos here. Dry leaves skip and skitter. A bare elm in the wind is a skeleton's pantomime. This whirling world.

My grandfather was born in Vilytsya, a village in present-day Ukraine, near the border with Poland and Belarus. He immigrated to the United States as a boy, then worked as a cook in the army, and after that in a restaurant in New Haven's Union Station. He died of leukemia while still in his 30s. My mother had a photograph but no memory of him.

His name was Gordya Gabriel Shulick. My grandmother's name was Sarah Anna McDermott. My mother's name was Helen Anna Shulick, but most people called her Nancy, after the little girl in the Sunday comics.

The New Haven Courthouse, where *Griswold v. Connecticut* would be heard in 1962, and Bobby Seale would go on trial in 1970, as protesters supporting the Black Panthers overflowed the Green, is a white marble pantheon built during the global catastrophe of World War I: the law as reason and proportion. On the steps sit two classical orators on tall plinths, their faces eroded from a century of acid rain.

My mother kept asking her mother where her father was. "There, that's your father!" the angry Irishwoman said, pointing to gray Cicero.

¤

In *Wallace Stevens: The Poems of Our Climate*, Bloom defines a visionary tradition in American poetry descending from Emerson through Whitman and Dickinson to Stevens. He uses Freud, Nietzsche, and the Kabbalah to theorize the disjunctions, silences, and absences he calls "poetic crossings."

Bloom was born in the Bronx, the youngest son in a family of Orthodox Jews. His father was a garment worker from Odessa. His mother came from Brest-Litovsk. His first language was Yiddish. As a child, his father gave him a small pair of shears to prepare him for his future occupation in the garment district.

Yale's tenured English professors gathered for a photo in 1967. All of them are white. Only two are Jews — Bloom and Charles Feidelson. Standing beside Bloom, on the edge of the group, is Pearson, who, with Feidelson, founded the American Studies program at Yale. Seated in the center is Marie Borroff, the one woman in the group and just the second woman tenured at Yale. Standing behind

her at six feet nine inches or more, with his arms crossed, is William K. Wimsatt. Wimsatt and Brooks had made Yale a center for the New Criticism. Their intellectual position, emulating T. S. Eliot's, was neoclassical, anti-Romantic, Anglophile, and Christian.

Bloom championed Stevens over Eliot, whom he despised for his antisemitism. Belonging to a generation of Jewish intellectuals who forged careers in the WASP-dominated academy, Bloom saw literature as a contest for cultural authority. As such, it was about power and rhetoric, and was written by people in history, with biographies.

After the New Criticism, this was an innovation. The fact that Bloom made the innovation at Yale was not an accident: his theory of literature emerged from his fight to produce it. He dedicated *The Anxiety of Influence* to Wimsatt. When Bloom was his student, Wimsatt returned his first paper "with the ringing comment, 'You are a Longinian critic, which I abhor!'" As could have been predicted from its thesis, *The Anxiety of Influence* opened a path for feminist and other political criticisms that were antithetical to Bloom's. He abhorred these developments theatrically and for so long it was easy to forget he had once been the iconoclast.

¤

First-year students enter Yale's Old Campus through Phelps Gate, facing the Green. Inside is a statue of Nathan Hale, the Yale College graduate who was hung as a spy by the British in 1776. Casts of the Hale statue stand at CIA Headquarters and the Department of Justice. The young man's back is straight, and his heels together. His ankles and fists are bound by

rope.

Nathaniel Jocelyn, a New Haven artist and abolitionist, and my great-great-grandfather, was commissioned by Robert Purvis, a Black abolitionist in Philadelphia, to paint an oil portrait of Joseph Cinqué. The painting was part of the campaign to sway opinion in favor of the Amistad rebels as their case went before the US Supreme Court. It depicts Cinqué gazing high and to his right, away from us. His expression is resolute yet mild. One shoulder is naked. Across his chest flows a soft, snowy robe, like a toga — a classicizing touch. In his fist is a cane pole: shepherd's staff or spear? There's an African landscape behind him. But that cliff looks like East Rock.

From Henry T. Blake's *Chronicles of New Haven Green* (1898):

The town government was finally organized October 25, 1639, and its first act was to try and convict an Indian named Nepaupuck for murder, which it did with alacrity and despatch. We read in the record of the trial that the culprit was arrested October 26, and set in the stocks. Before that time therefore the stocks and doubtless the whipping post had been erected on the market place; and thus these emblems of Christian civilization were the earliest tokens of its dedication to free institutions and public enjoyment. Four days later, that is on October 30, 1639, as the record tersely informs us, "the Indian's head was cut off and pitched upon a pole in the market place," this being the second step in the improvement of the Green and the first attempt to put a cheerful face upon the public pleasure ground.

Just now, as I read that book on my laptop, a hand flashed across the screen — the hand of the library worker who scanned it. Dark brown skin, pink close-bitten nails, the knuckles' wrinkles, fine black hairs, the fan-shaped bones. A hand, pressing on the page.

In 2018, parents and children unpacked their SUVs, and carried laptops, lacrosse sticks, and Ikea furniture through Phelps Gate while across College Street, in view of the Taft Hotel, police and paramedics huddled around motionless bodies on the Green, lying there like piles of leaves, or souls refused at the Second Coming. Local hospitals treated more than 100 people for drug overdoses that day. Two Americas, one street.

¤

In his lifelong effort to articulate a secular vision of ultimate reality, Stevens wrote his poetry in conscious opposition to Eliot and the poets and critics influenced by him. Perhaps that hostility was behind his guilty fantasy that he had insulted Brooks and his wife. Although shy, Stevens, like Bloom, was pugnacious.

Canto XII of "An Ordinary Evening in New Haven" had special importance for Bloom. He wrote about it on several occasions over the course of his career, each time tracing the trope of fallen leaves back in literary history from Whitman, Shelley, Milton, Dante, and Virgil to Homer — marble men on the white courthouse steps he called *The Western Canon*.

The poem is the cry of its occasion,

Part of the res itself and not about it.
The poet speaks the poem as it is,

Not as it was: part of the reverberation
Of a windy night as it is, when the marble statues
Are like newspapers blown by the wind. He speaks

By sight and insight as they are. There is no
Tomorrow for him. The wind will have passed by,
The statues will have gone back to be things about.

The mobile and the immobile flickering
In the area between is and was are leaves,
Leaves burnished in autumnal burnished trees

And leaves in whirlings in the gutters, whirlings
Around and away, resembling the presence of thought,
Resembling the presence of thoughts, as if,

In the end, in the whole psychology, the self,
The town, the weather, in a casual litter,
Together, said words of the world are the life of the world.

Bloom liked to argue from word-roots, as if the whole history of a word were present in every use of it. About "the cry of its occasion," he says:

An occasion is an event or

happening, but its etymological meaning is a falling down, and its Indo-European root means falling *or* dying. To be the cry of fallen leaves is to be a cry in the etymological sense of crying out or imploring the aid of one's fellow citizens ("cry" is from the Latin *quiritare*, in turn from *quiris* for a Roman citizen).

Section 47 of "Of the Leaves that Have Fallen" begins with a "quick incision. A cut." Severed "[c]lose but not / Too close to the base," "the boy's penis unlocks like a votive door in which leaves / Fly out, falling, and, historical, also having fallen." These leaves cry out, imploring their fellow citizens to come to their aid. But the white people gathered in the photos Laurentiis is writing about have come to see a boy hang, swaying from a tree or a bridge, over and over, at the center of town, or somewhere in the woods. "To navigate the dark, you must listen, you must listen / To the dark: the wind, a wind in the trees…"

"Wallace Stevens," Laurentiis says in an interview, "is probably my favorite poet, certainly my favorite Modernist poet."

¤

Although he won the Bollingen Prize (1949), National Book Award (twice, in 1951 and 1955), and Pulitzer Prize (1955), it was only in the 1970s, when his poetry began to be widely taught in colleges and universities, that Stevens gained the canonical status we take for granted for him today.

It is disorienting when "[t]he poet speaks the poem as it is," rather than as past poems prescribe. Something new has come into the world, and nothing will be the same again. Even the past has been changed. Soon, however, perhaps as early as tomorrow, "The statues will have gone back to be things about": objects you walk past, here and there, without really seeing.

In 2016, New Haven prosecutors dismissed charges against Corey Menafee, who was employed as a dishwasher in what was then known as Calhoun College, one of Yale's residential colleges, located on the northwest corner of the Green. When it opened in 1933, the college was named in honor of the "cast-iron" defender of the "positive good" of chattel slavery, John C. Calhoun. After years of controversy, in 2017, the college was renamed for a computer scientist and US rear admiral, Grace Murray Hopper.

Menafee had been arrested for destroying a stained-glass window in the dining hall, a window depicting slaves picking cotton. "I took a broomstick," he said, "and it was kind of high, and I climbed up and reached up and broke it."

¤

Roger Gilbert was a PhD student when I was. His dissertation became a book called *Walks in the World*, which identifies a genre central to American poetry, the walk-poem. "For Stevens," Roger writes, "the walk provides not a narrative armature but an occasion, an experiential node out of which the poem's 'never-ending meditation' flows. That occasion in turn shapes the vision of the poem, which finds motion or traversal to be the ultimate form of reality."

My mother was 14. A Wednesday afternoon in September. Her dog Lucky had taken the bus to meet her — the driver knew Lucky. They were waiting on the

Green to take the bus home after school when the sky grew dark and strange, clouds whirled the wrong way, and the 1938 Hurricane, the most devastating storm in state history, roared ashore a few miles east of New Haven. It must have felt like the end of the world.

The apocalypse in canto XII of "An Ordinary Evening in New Haven" is natural and historical, not Christian. The storm of time blows away all judges and orators — statues that tumble across the street like newspapers. When the wind blows through the factory's windows, the poet's pages are leaves "whirling," falling "between is and was." Inner and outer worlds have the same fate, blown away "in a casual litter." Letters become litter.

In 2012, a woman, who was homeless and living on the Green, discovered a human skull in the roots of a tree blown over by a hurricane. The jaw was open as if to cry out, but crammed with dirt. The bones had been there probably since the 17th century, when the Puritans consecrated the city's first cemetery. Remember, when you cross the Green, you are walking over thousands of skeletons.

¤

Ultimate reality as "traversal." The image comes from the final lines of "An Ordinary Evening in New Haven":

These are the edgings and inch-
  ings of final form,
The swarming activities of the
  formulae
Of statement, directly and indirectly getting at,

Like an evening evoking the
  spectrum of violet,

A philosopher practicing scales
  on his piano,
A woman writing a note and
  tearing it up.

It is not in the premise that reality
Is a solid. It may be a shade that
  traverses
A dust, a force that traverses a
  shade.

Edging, inching, swarming: Stevens's participles evoke a reality that is virtual because always in motion, somewhere up ahead or just behind us. That phrase "directly and indirectly getting at" has no object; there is only the "getting at." The man in the physical streets of New Haven is a passerby, a metaphysical shade traversing the dust of this place, himself the dust that a force is passing across and beyond. Nothing solid. Shadows walking, crossing over and on.

Narumi Nekpenekpen, *sugar plum.basketball*, 2020. Courtesy the artist and Deli Gallery, NY.

GAPS AND ASTERISKS

LOUISA HALL

Two recently published novels about life in the age of the internet — Lauren Oyler's *Fake Accounts* and Patricia Lockwood's *No One Is Talking About This* — address the question of what they see as a recent surge in broken prose: books written in essayistic bits, separated by gaps or asterisks. The style, both books claim, is particularly contemporary. Oyler's narrator dislikes it; Lockwood's narrator — who writes in that style — remains more ambivalent.

In *Fake Accounts*:

Having read several [of these fragmented books] because they were easy to finish, I couldn't help but object: this trendy style was melodramatic, insinuating utmost meaning where there was only hollow prose, and in its attempts to reflect the world as a sequence of distinct and clearly formed ideas, it ran counter to how reality actually worked. Especially, I had to assume, if you had a baby, which is a purposeful experience (don't let it die) but also chaotic (it might die). Since the interviewer and the author agreed there was something distinctly feminine about this style, I felt guilty admitting it, but I saw no other choice: I did not like the style.

In *No One Is Talking About This*:

Why were we all writing like this now? Because a new kind of connection had to be made, and blink, synapse, little space-between was the only way to make it. Or because, and this was more frightening, it was the way the portal wrote.

In *Fake Accounts*, it is a (bad) form often chosen by women. In *No One Is Talking About This*, it is a form chosen by millennials whose prose has been influenced by the alienation of the internet age and an adulthood steeped in the language of tweets. In both, it is definitely/probably a regrettable development.

¤

Prose broken to bits by gaps and/or asterisks is not, of course, a new development. In 2010, David Shields wrote a manifesto broken with many gaps and asterisks and demanding that all prose henceforth be broken by gaps and asterisks. 2010 is

a long time ago in the internet age, but the examples Shields gives of exemplary literature broken by gaps and asterisks date back very much further: the lists and accounts that were the earliest forms of writing in 3200 BCE; the *Iliad* and the *Odyssey*, 800 BCE; Sumerian anthologies of aphorism; Plutarch's essays; Anne Bradstreet's letters; Emerson's essays; Kafka's notebooks; *Speedboat* (1976) and *Sleepless Nights* (1979), both novels composed out of fragments.

It wasn't uncommon, in the 20th century, for novels to be broken by gaps and/or asterisks: *Cane*, the 1923 novel by Jean Toomer, is a novel broken by frequent gaps. *Margery Kempe* (1994), by Robert Glück, is a novel broken by gaps. *The Savage Detectives* and *2666* are both novels broken by frequent gaps and asterisks. Twentieth-century nonfiction was also very commonly broken by gaps and asterisks: *The Motion of Light in Water* by Samuel Delany; many essays by Annie Dillard; *Dora Bruder* by Patrick Modiano; *The Book of Embraces* by Eduardo Galeano.

One small way of thinking about poetry in any century is that it is prose broken by gaps and asterisks. Novels-in-verse are broken by gaps and asterisks; diaries are broken by gaps and asterisks; novels in the form of diaries are broken by gaps and asterisks; epistolary novels are broken by gaps and asterisks. Commonplace books — from E. M. Forster's to Ross Gay's recent *The Book of Delights* — have always been broken by gaps and asterisks.

And so on. It seems likely to me that a writer now who chooses to break their books with gaps and asterisks would be likely to be as influenced by any of these ancient traditions as they would be by Twitter or the internet or even recent exemplary books (*Citizen*, *Motherhood*,

The Argonauts) broken by gaps and/or asterisks.

¤

Given such a long and storied tradition, what to make of Lockwood's narrator's anxiety and Oyler's narrator's disdain?

Oyler's narrator's disdain is easier to investigate because it is allied with Oyler's own, as expressed in a review of Eula Biss's *Having and Being Had*, which she describes as a book "composed of anecdotes, miniature histories and cultural criticism that make up essays a page or two long."

One of her complaints about the form is that it is vague: "[T]here is a sense that Biss is after something specific, even if she doesn't know what it is. Metaphors are tested, ironies pressed upon. Etymologies abound."

Another one of her complaints is that the form borrows — inexpertly — from the real experts:

[S]ome sections seem almost entirely composed of quotations and paraphrases; the contemporary scholars Lewis Hyde, Alison Light and David Graeber, among others, are cited so often that it seems part of Biss's plan to buy time had to involve stealing it from other writers. Curated nonfiction is popular now for the way it seems to fit with collectivist politics; while reading it I always reach a point at which I wish I were reading the books being extensively quoted.

Another complaint has to do with all the white space: a rip-off for the reader who has purchased it.

So: Trendy, melodramatic, and counter-to-reality, and also vague, plagiaristic, and inflated. But are epistolary novels — which are also broken by gaps, and often composed of jostling and essayistic fragments — trendy, melodramatic, counter-to-reality, etc.? Are novels in verse, are commonplace books, is poetry? These, it seems to me, are questions of how the form is used, and perhaps how the form is received (what was expected of it, and what was missed as a result), not flaws inherent in the form itself.

¤

Another one of Oyler's complaints in her review of Biss's book has to do with the feeling that Biss has promised a book about class and instead delivered one about herself: "What she's serious about, it slowly comes to seem, is her own life and how to live it."

This anger at an author who has promised to write about a subject and has instead written about her own shifting relationship to that subject reminds me of a series of scathing reviews I recently read about Ann Beattie's *Mrs. Nixon: A Novelist Imagines a Life*, another book composed of small, jostling fragments.

In *The New York Times*, Michiko Kakutani wrote:

The title of Ann Beattie's new book, *Mrs. Nixon: A Novelist Imagines a Life*, suggests that the author might be trying to channel Pat Nixon, or conjure up her life with Dick, much the way Curtis Sittenfeld channeled a Laura Bush-like first lady in her 2008 novel, "American Wife."

It turns out, however, that Ms. Beattie isn't really much interested in Mrs. Nixon or her life at the White House or her more-than-five-decade-long marriage. Rather, she's interested in deconstructing this famously opaque former-first-lady as a sort of literary exercise — to test her own skills as a writer and to find an excuse to blather on (and on and on) about her own ideas about fiction writing, about women, and about the interface between life and art.

The Washington Post's review, entitled "Self-absorbed Mrs. Nixon: It's All About Ann Beattie," complains that, "Mrs. Nixon is ostensibly a novel about the first lady, and yet it hardly engages Pat Nixon at all."

But did these reviewers open Mrs. Nixon: A Novelist Imagines a Life and think they were opening a biography? Did they want to open a biography? Did they think a novel is and should be a biography?

If you expected a book by Ann Beattie called Mrs. Nixon: A Novelist Imagines a Life to be a biography of Pat Nixon, I can imagine you would feel disappointed when you read it (though even that disappointment, I think, would be misguided: even that ur-biography, Boswell's Life of Samuel Johnson, is — as the title makes clear — as much about Boswell as it is about Samuel Johnson).

But if you don't expect a novel to be a biography (or a work of creative nonfiction to be a lecture delivered on a particular subject), and instead expect a novel (or a work of creative nonfiction) to be about the mind of the author in relationship to its subject, then you would read its form (in these cases shifting, impermanent,

relational, plagiaristic) as an expression of the states of mind of the author, and not a statement about a particular subject. And in that case, all the little parts, broken by spaces, would be the form the author chose to represent how her mind moved around the particular subject.

¤

Why would a writer choose to write a book full of gaps and asterisks? Oyler suggests that it permits the author to lean on (and steal from) sharper minds; her narrator in Fake Accounts suggests that it lends profundity where there is none. Lockwood's narrator fears it isn't the writer who chooses the form, but rather the internet, expressing itself through the writer. The woman Oyler's narrator mocks suggests that she chose the form because she is a busy mother.

These all seem like believable enough reasons why a writer might choose a form. Conditions of production are important — Grace Paley famously said that she wrote short stories (and not long novels) because she was a mother and an activist and "art is long and life is short." It isn't only mothers (or parents, or caregivers of any kind) who are too busy to write endless novels: anyone with a difficult job is too busy to write endless novels without taking breaks, as is anyone with a difficult life.

A lot of exposure to tweets also seems like an interesting reason to try a novel broken up into bits; so does a fear that one's mind isn't sharp enough or profound enough on its own, and the desire to incorporate sharper and more profound bits into one's consciousness.

Writerly pleasure also seems like a good reason, to me. It's pleasing, when you come to the end of an idea, to congratulate yourself with two brisk hits to the space bar, a resounding shift-eight, and then another two hits on the space bar.

In "The Changing View of Man in the Portrait," John Berger suggests a slew of more interesting and more important reasons:

> We hear a lot about the crisis of the modern novel. What this involves, fundamentally, is a change in the mode of narration. It is scarcely any longer possible to tell a straight story sequentially unfolding in time. And this is because we are too aware of what is continually traversing the story line laterally. That is to say, instead of being aware of a point as an infinitely small part of a straight line, we are aware of it as an infinitely small part of an infinite number of lines, as the centre of a star of lines. Such awareness is the result of our constantly having to take into account the simultaneity and extension of events and possibilities.

There are many reasons why this should be so: the range of modern means of communication: the scale of modern power: the degree of personal political responsibility that must be accepted for events all over the world: the fact that the world has become indivisible: the unevenness of economic development within that world: the scale of the exploitation.

He talks about Cubism as an attempt to paint a portrait with an awareness of "having to take into account the simultaneity and extension of events and possibilities." A prose broken by gaps and asterisks, in which the perspective shifts slightly with every break, seems like another approach to the same problem.

In *Reality Hunger*, David Shields gives other reasons for choosing the form. He quotes (or specifically does not quote, theft of bits and pieces from other minds being an important part of the art for which he advocates) Alain Robbe-Grillet, who describes the form as a choice that stands against old-fashioned narrative, which — he says — is a relic of 19th-century aristocracy ("The world's destiny has ceased, for us, to be identified with the rise and fall of certain men, of certain families").

Elsewhere he describes it as more representative of actual psychology ("While we tend to conceive of the operations of the mind as unified and transparent, they're actually chaotic and opaque. There's no invisible boss in the brain, no central meaner, no unitary self in command of our activities and utterances") and also more representative of the actual world ("Conventional fiction teaches the reader that life is a coherent, fathomable whole that concludes in neatly wrapped-up revelation. Life, though — standing on a street corner, channel surfing, trying to navigate the web or a declining relationship, hearing that a close friend died last night — flies at us in bright splinters").

I can imagine a manifesto that describes a prose form full of gaps in a way that is similar to Denise Levertov's description of "exploratory poetry": "What I mean by that word is that such poetry, more than most poetry of the past, incorporates and reveals the *process* of thinking/feeling, feeling/thinking, rather than focusing more exclusively on its *results*." The most crucial tool for this, she says, is the line break, which records the hesitations between words that cannot be recorded by normal punctuation, a hesitation which — she suggests — marks the moment when the mind has questioned the line it has just uttered, or slightly adjusted its stance. Perhaps a prose full of gaps is a prose full of such pauses that exist outside of and in addition to punctuation.

Or one that imagines a prose form full of gaps along the lines that Harryette Mullen describes in the preface to her collection *Urban Tumbleweed*, a book of episodic verses broken by gaps that she describes as a tanka diary:

> [T]he brevity and clarity of tanka make it suitable for capturing in concise form the ephemera of everyday life. With refined awareness of seasonal changes and a classical repertoire of fleeting impressions, Japanese traditional poetry contemplates, among other things, the human being's place in the natural world, an idea I wanted to explore in my own nontraditional way.

Perhaps a prose style full of white space is also well suited for showing the ways in which ephemera break upon us and then pass, the fleeting way the natural world intersects with consciousness.

Or one that describes a prose form full of gaps in a way that is similar to Helen Vendler's description of poetry that features a break in the poet's style:

> When a poet puts off an old style (to speak for a moment as though this were a deliberate undertaking), he or she perpetrates an act of violence, so to speak, on the self. It is not too much to say that the old body must be dematerialized if the poet is to assume a new one. [...] The fears and regrets attending the act of permanent stylistic change can be understood by analogy with divorce, expatriation, and other such painful spiritual or imaginative departures. It is hoped, of course, that the new body — like the new spouse or the new country — will be more satisfactory than the old, but it is a hope, not a certainty.

Perhaps a prose style full of gaps and asterisks is a style that enacts all the small (and large) violences we do against ourselves in daily life, all the ways we wrench ourselves from one thought, or one marriage, or one home, or one country, into the next.

Or one that imagines a prose form full of gaps as a strategy for foregrounding the daily, cumulative process of writing, the way the practice of a form not only represents the mind, but changes the mind that has chosen to use it — something along the lines of what Ross Gay describes in his preface to *The Book of Delights*:

> I came up with a handful of rules: write a delight every day for a year; begin and end on my birthday, August 1; draft them quickly; and write them by hand. The rules made it a discipline for me. A practice. Spend time thinking and writing about delight every day. [...] It didn't take me long to learn that the discipline or practice of writing these essays occasioned a kind of delight radar.

Or maybe it was more like the development of a delight muscle. Something that implies that the more you study delight, the more delight there is to study.

Or I can imagine a manifesto that describes a prose form full of gaps in a way that is similar to Jim Ferris's "The Enjambed Body: A Step Toward a Crippled Poetics," an essay itself full of gaps and asterisks that calls us to eschew our love of evenness and regularity and value, instead, a limping poetics. Perhaps a prose style full of gaps and asterisks is just that: a limping prose style, composed of irregular parts, parts irregular enough to represent our irregular bodies and lives.

There are a lot of interesting reasons I can imagine to break up prose with gaps and asterisks, and a lot I haven't managed to imagine yet. It's probably impossible to come up with a single, unifying aesthetic theory for a form that has been with us since the beginning of writing, and that basically consists of alternating white space with black space, except to say that it is not a new form, not a form that can be claimed by the internet, not a form that can be claimed by anyone, not a form that is either good or bad. It is only a form that only promises to have many different beginnings and many different endings, to contain many different attempts at expression, and so seems like a good form for representing the ceaseless movement of a mind coming into contact with a subject it knows it hasn't mastered yet.

ALL-AMERICAN GHAZAL

DUJIE TAHAT

I'm long past angry and, yes, beyond tired, I wish I could say
but they're just kids and my girlfriend's watching. I could pray

at dawn, at dusk, a few more unfoldings, a thousand sun
lit hours. But I don't. I won't. I yell and they stop playing,

look down at their bare feet, log onto class. There is nothing
about these days that resembles ritual. Oh, I have been played

too — flayed myself in the furious pause of a father's hesitation —
for show, toyed with like the fraying fringe of fake praying.

I left the church over my mother's protestation, even after
the cathedral burned down, yet found myself in another prayer.

A tongue tides along my trim to forget, for a second, the volume
of forgiveness. I've hid in many stairwells. I slide a bead along, say

a bit of something familiar: *Alhamdu* — but it doesn't come as easy
as it did once. The thing about Eros is: I love being bitter. Salt prey

after the hunt. Salinity is close to divinity. *Hail Mary.* My God
got a well rounded pallet, an appetite I can fuck with. Every lover I

have ever had has said something about the way I eat. Hollow
leg. How I can pick a whole fried tilapia to its cones. I suck its eyes

and its cheeks. If we're talking about sex, my kids are still here.
There is a body before a body. Legs. More legs. Afraid to pray,

or maybe to ruin the moment of entering, I take off my shoes, before
knocking, wash my elbows, ears, rinse my name, Dujie: say it.

Kayla Ephros, *spells and charms*, 2020, graphite on paper, 8.5 x 11 inches. Courtesy of the artist.

DOING JUSTICE TO EGYPTIAN FEMINISTS

RAPHAEL CORMACK

I am a white man who has written a book about women of color. Over the course of writing *Midnight in Cairo*, a nonfiction book exploring the lives and experiences of some of the most powerful and charismatic women of Cairo's early 20th-century nightlife, several issues arose which I could not ignore. The lives of women like these have so often been misrepresented by men like me.

It was not what I set out to do. With more vanity I'd imagine the subject chose me, but in fact I stumbled upon it in the course of my PhD research on Arabic adaptations of Sophocles's *Oedipus Tyrannus*. As I was looking through the old theatrical magazine and microfilmed copies of newspapers, I found myself drawn into page after page of vivid stories of the actresses, singers, and dancers, whose performances — and lives off-stage — had clearly riveted many readers before me, spawning dozens of celebrity interviews and full-length memoirs. There were women who had started their own cabarets, theater troupes, and film companies. Practical feminists who faced up to patriarchy and British imperialism. They were almost totally unknown outside the Middle East, but with every new source I found tantalizing new snippets of their lives and details of their careers. It is a truism in historical writing that before around 1950, you have to make an effort to uncover women's voices amid the cacophony of self-important men. But in Cairo's interwar nightlife scene, they were everywhere. It would be impossible to tell the story of Egypt's roaring '20s without them.

I wanted to bring these women to new audiences but I had genuine concerns. The time when self-declared "experts" (usually white men like me) could write whatever they wanted without having to answer to anyone else except a small group of other self-declared "experts" (who are also white men) is coming to an end. It has been a privilege to try and bring the material I have found to light, but one that must come with responsibilities.

Writing about other cultures can go very wrong. In 1922, the eccentric pulp fiction writer Achmed Abdullah (whose family background, which allegedly includes both Afghan and Russian aristocracy, is complicated enough to warrant a whole article), published a scathing review of the new Cambridge History of India. In part he was attacking its turgid academic style. "There exists a type of academic mind which soaks itself in facts as a

sponge drinks water," he began. "Press the sponge, and the water squirts out, a little more muddy, a little more stale." The review went on: "This History of India is as platitudinously impressive as a Methodist bishop. It reaches that apex of good breeding: a complete vacuity of soul."

But it was not only the lifeless academic style that annoyed Abdullah. The almost-scientific attempts of these "Anglo-Saxon" scholars to understand India were doomed to failure. The book, he said, "looks at the great peninsula through blue spectacles. These spectacles are eminently well-fitted, eminently practical. But they focus wrong when used to look beyond Boston, Regent Street, and the pleasant Downs of Sussex-by-the-Sea."

These "blue spectacles" that Abdullah talks about probably refer to the colored lenses that travelers wore in sunny countries before sunglasses were invented. Foreign tourists in Egypt cut a strange figure, with their blue or green spectacles and muslin over their face to protect themselves from the outside. There was also a striking metaphor in their appearance. As Timothy Mitchell says, they were trying to "see without being seen," to observe from within a sealed capsule.

The problem of the "Western" gaze on the "East" was influentially dissected by Edward Said in *Orientalism*. There, he argued that a whole host of writers who claimed (and often believed) that they were writing their honest, impartial observations motivated by nothing but curiosity, were really participating in the creation of an image in the Middle East as a part of the world that was separate and opposed to the "West" and, by extension, ripe for colonization. One of Said's most influential and important arguments was that the construction of the "East," which motivated so much European imperialism, did not just come from within the halls of power but from supposedly unaffiliated writers. You can almost feel his disappointment as he finds that writers that he otherwise admires (Flaubert, for instance) turn their eyes to the Middle East and end up repeating the same old, false clichés.

Edward Said's ghost hung heavy over me as I wrote my book, not least because he himself had written two short articles about one of the women I feature: the belly dancer, actress, and underground left-wing, anti-imperialist activist Tahiyya Carioca. Said described his sexual awakening at the age of 14, when he saw her dance at a nightclub in Cairo. But, I have not only written a history of the Middle East, I have written about the women of the region, not just as a "Westerner" but as a man. I am open to the charge that I can never fully understand the experiences of the women whose stories I tell in the book.

The women I write about themselves were aware of the problems of men telling their stories for them. Fatima Sirri, one of the many successful singers and actresses in 1920s Cairo, spent almost a decade involved in a lawsuit with a man to recognize his paternity — the first case of its kind in Egypt. She eventually won, sustained in large part by the money she made as a singer, but as the case was still going on, she published her own detailed account of the birth of the child and her failed relationship with the father. She knew the kind of things that men were saying about her and went on the offensive. "All you male authors who write about the female psyche, not one of you has ever been a woman, so how can you know anything about the female psyche?"

In 1920, the feminist writer May Ziadeh published a biography of her fellow activist Malak Hifni Nasif in Cairo. In the book, Ziadeh printed some correspondence she had exchanged with the subject of the book. She makes almost the exactly same point as Fatima Sirri would a few years later:

> Whether he is writing a general study or turning his pen to specifics, a man cannot shed light on female emotion because he writes with his intellect, his egotism, and his severity and a woman lives with her heart, her emotions, and her love. Only a doctor who knows our terrible diseases can treat them. A woman knows what ails her sex so she is the one who will cure it.

So where does my work stand in light of all these warnings? What would the women I write about feel about it?

Can it even stand at all?

In *Orientalism*, Said makes it very clear that he does not think that people in Europe or America can no longer write history about the Middle East. His project was, at its core, a humanist one. One of his central criticisms of the stereotyped, imperial, and dangerous intellectual construction of an "Orient" fundamentally opposed to the West was that it has stood in the way of a true attempts at cross-cultural dialogue and understanding. In an introduction to a later edition of the book, he clearly states that it is not the study of or interest in different cultures that is the problem, but how that interest can reinforce systems of power and supremacy. There is, he says, "a profound difference between the will to understand for purposes of co-existence and humanistic enlargement of horizons, and the will to dominate for the purposes of control and external dominion."

So, if it is possible for someone like me, as a humanist committed to the enlargement of horizons, to write a book like this, the next important question becomes: *How* should it be done? How can we acknowledge the problems that exist in the project but also attempt to transcend them (at least to a degree) and reach what Said called "the common enterprise of promoting human community"?

The first of my strategies was to try to ensure that the women in my book are allowed to speak for themselves, nothing more and nothing less. Using their own words and their own memoirs wherever possible, supplemented by contemporary sources, I have tried to reproduce their lives as faithfully as possible. I hope that, were these women alive, they would recognize themselves in the book.

But, equally, I do not want to use their individual stories as a way to make grand claims which they cannot support. Part of the curse of living in the Middle East is that everything you do is seen as an explanation for some huge geopolitical or religious problem. Individual stories are asked to carry the weight of representing the entirety of a culture or a religion. The stories in my book are windows into Egypt's culture and nightlife in the early 20th century, but I don't claim they will explain an entire part of the world in all its facets.

Secondly, no book is the work of just one person. Not even this article is the work of one person. I would never have seen Achmed Abdullah's review if the scholar Esmat Elhalaby had not shown it to me. Over the course of working on *Midnight in Cairo*, I have realized just how much I have been shaped by female intellectuals. Since the first time I lived in Egypt in 2010, I have had the generous support and friendship of many academics who took the time to help me. Early in my journey two great female scholars of Egyptian theater, Nehad Selaiha and Iman Ezzeldin, gave me both their time and some of their books (no small thing for an academic). Nehad Selaiha died in 2017 but her work has continued to be an inspiration, especially her book which feature a long chapter on Fatima Sirri's long court case and its ramifications.

While writing my book I reread *May Her Likes Be Multiplied*, a study of Arab women's life writing from the 19th and 20th centuries by my PhD supervisor, Marilyn Booth, I was struck by how much it had influenced my own thinking. Many of my thoughts on performance and drama are deeply indebted to my other PhD supervisor, Olga Taxidou. As I wrote the book, I discovered how much my mother, classicist Mary Beard, had left her mark on me — from her attempts to move beyond great men, generals, and battles and get a sense of the everyday, to her insistence on deconstructing often repeated myths little supported by close reading of sources and her demonstration of the ways women have been silenced throughout history. *Midnight in Cairo* is really the product of countless scholars, writers, and friends in Egypt and elsewhere, whose contributions I have always tried to acknowledge. In the course of research, I was also introduced to and influenced by Cairo's amazing HaRaKa collective, a dance collective who is currently doing performances based on the history of Cairo's early 20th-century cabarets, and Heschek Beschek, a group of female performers from Egypt and other nations based in Berlin.

Finally, I have tried to create space rather than take it up. Publishing does not have to be a zero-sum game and if *Midnight in Cairo* leads to more interest in the unknown histories of women, there are many books just waiting to be translated into English. Lamia Ziadé's wonderful, illustrated history of the 20th-century Arabic entertainment business, *Ya Ain, Ya Layl*, still has no English edition. Likewise, Salah Isa's rich and deeply researched *Rijal Raya wa-Sakina*, the story of two Alexandrian sex workers-turned-murderers which is also one of the great works of modern Arabic social history, has also never been translated into English. As far as I am aware, there is not even an English edition of any works by May Ziadeh, one of the most eloquent Arab feminists of the 20th century. There is a very deep well of amazing stories from the Arab world waiting to find new audiences.

We are moving into a new age. With it, the world is opening up to a whole new set of stories. What my place is in this new world, I am not sure. In the end, I will not be the one to judge whether my own attempts to write a history have avoided the mistakes of the past. But whatever my book's reception, I am looking forward to a continuing shake-up in history writing and the long neglected and forgotten stories that it will uncover.

Narumi Nekpenekpen, *star spanker*, 2020. Courtesy the artist and Deli Gallery, NY.

ON MICHAEL S. HARPER, "DEAR JOHN, DEAR COLTRANE" (1966)

EDWARD HIRSCH

Michael Harper wrote about family and friends, about iconic figures from the American pantheon, his personal pantheon, which spanned the centuries. It included a host of poets and musicians, of course, but also historical figures — Roger Williams, John Brown, Martin Luther King Jr., Jackie Robinson — all of them representative presences, exemplars who tried to wake us from the nightmares of American history. Ralph Ellison said that "while one can do nothing about choosing one's relatives, one can, as artist, choose one's ancestors," and that's precisely what Harper did. He looked for connection and elevation, inspiring heroes. He may have considered himself an eccentric, but he also called his selected poems *Images of Kin*, and extended the idea of kinship, which for him consisted of bonding and recognition, a sort of chosen family of lineage and ancestry. He believed in songlines and pathways, in the American continuum, in learning history from oral tradition and library archives — he argued that American poets needed to be better archivists — and he wove his personal story into a national tapestry. He despised injustice and countered it with his own idiosyncratic eloquence. Above all, he believed in poetry and music, modes of comparative humanity, and found solace in art.

Harper was determined to situate himself as both a Black and an American poet. He was capacious in his reading, his enthusiasms, and unapologetic about his love for John Keats and Robert Frost — his own work has a Keatisian intensity, a Frostian feeling for vernacular eloquence. He adopted two literary fathers, Sterling A. Brown and Robert Hayden, and celebrated their work with a relentless sense of mission at a time when they were often scorned and condescended to by the Black Arts Movement. More than anyone else, he helped bring them back into the family archive. He loved their work not just because they were consummate poets but also because they were moral historians. He appreciated the way Brown had kept the folk spirit alive in African American poetry, the way he had built his own work on the dignity of folk forms, such as blues, work songs, spirituals, and folktales. Brown's commitment to the exceptional in the commonplace fueled Harper's project. So, too, Harper admired Hayden's perfect pitch as a poet, his succinctness and sincerity, his unearthing of crucial American sources, his essential humanity. In his poem "Healing Song,"

he characterized Hayden as "this creature of transcendence / a love-filled shadow, congealed and clarified."

Harper loved two art forms equally, jazz and poetry, and took consolation from both. Jazz came first and initiated him into poetry. He noted that he never would have become a poet if his family hadn't moved from Brooklyn to West Los Angeles when he was 13 years old. He went to high school and college in L.A. The Angeleno poet Henri Coulette taught and encouraged him at California State University, Los Angeles, where he also took classes with Christopher Isherwood, who introduced him to another early influence and inspiration, W. H. Auden. Nurtured on the California jazz scene, Harper was surrounded by a group of highly talented musicians who shaped his sensibility — and he admitted that he would have liked to become a musician, but he never had the chops. It's not just that he took the rhythmic beat, the pulse of his poems, from jazz, but also that he got his emotional education from the music. He grew up on the big bands of Duke Ellington, Count Basie, Andy Kirk, Jimmie Lunceford, and Fletcher Henderson, and listened closely to jazz singers like Bessie Smith, Billie Holiday, and Mamie Smith. Most fundamentally, he witnessed the revolutionary change to bebop.

Harper was friends with McCoy Tyner, who was Coltrane's pianist, and he often attended live performances of Coltrane's four-piece band in the 1950s and '60s. He nominated Coltrane as his Orpheus and wrote poems about him all through his life. Coltrane's music sang to him, and so too did Coltrane's changed notion of the role of the artist, his rejection of minstrelsy in any form, his serious spiritual quest. Coltrane unabashedly transfigured pain into love and made love archetypal. That was the model.

Coltrane wasn't just a spiritual person; he was also a committed political one. Part of what Harper learned from him was how a major artist responded to racism and genocide, how he countered it with an awareness of Black identity and solidarity. With Harper in mind, it's worth listening again to Coltrane's song "Alabama," a requiem for the four girls murdered in the Ku Klux Klan's terrorist bombing of the 16th Street Baptist Church in Birmingham, Alabama, in 1963. It's also a response to Martin Luther King Jr.'s eulogy. The way that Coltrane responded to Dr. King's rhetoric became the basis for Harper's later poem, "Here Where Coltrane Is," which invokes a structure of feeling, the political and historical dimensions of Black art.

Harper wrote "Dear John, Dear Coltrane" in 1966, the year before Coltrane died. It's as if he intuited Coltrane's nearness to death. There's an element of magical thinking in his fear that he was signing a death warrant by creating an elegy in advance. He published the poem as the title piece in his first book in 1970, and it's been read as a retrospective ever since. I read it 50 years ago and still think of it as Harper's signature piece. He took the refrain line from Coltrane's album *A Love Supreme*, which was recorded in 1964 and released the next year. In one take, Trane led his regular quartet — pianist McCoy Tyner, bassist Jimmy Garrison, drummer Elvin Jones — through a suite in four parts. The title appears as a vocal chant in the first section, "Acknowledgement." Coltrane uses his tenor sax to play the opening four-note motif in all the keys, wringing dozens of changes out of it until

it turns into words intoned by Coltrane and the other musicians. It's as if he's using his preternatural musical dexterity to suggest that all musical paths lead to God. *A Love Supreme* has a spiritual grandeur that is rare in any era, but especially in modern times. It stands beside Rainer Maria Rilke's *Duino Elegies* and T. S. Eliot's *Four Quartets*, but is realized by four voices, by four different musicians.

By the time Harper wrote his poem, the phrase "a love supreme" had already become a tag line, a sort of anthem or refrain, not just in Los Angeles but in Black and musical communities all over the country. Harper's poem weds the jazz lyric to the verse epistle. He takes a tradition inaugurated by Langston Hughes, who used the syncopated rhythms and repetitive phrases of 1920s jazz as a way to address the struggles of African American life, and connects it to the philosophical letter poem, which has a much older provenance, dating back to Horace's *Epistles*. The title of Harper's poem, "Dear John, Dear Coltrane," is a double take. The poem is a meditation on Coltrane's life that poses as a letter to the musician, and, like all verse epistles, it's meant to be overheard by the rest of us.

Unlike any letter I've ever read, the poem divides the addressee's name into two parts. It's as if the poet is both writing a love letter, "Dear John," and also writing to someone he admires from a more formal distance, a symbolic figure, "Dear Coltrane." It's a proto-elegy. The title is the first indication of the importance of phrasing in the poem; indeed, as the title poem in Harper's first book, it points to the key lesson he learned from musicians. The phrasing itself seems to lead the artist somewhere he doesn't necessarily want to go. But that's precisely where he needs to go. Here, the title stammers and then jump cuts to the italicized and indented refrain of the poem, which seems chanted in Coltrane's own voice. This is the inaugural movement of the poem, and it's imperative to hear it four times:

a love supreme, a love supreme
a love supreme, a love supreme

Coltrane's music was addressed to God; Harper's poem is addressed to Coltrane. I think it has an erotic undercurrent ("I loved John Coltrane and I loved his music") and a religious overtone. There is a jolted jump, a serious downward turn, from the elevated refrain to the first brutal narrative section of the poem. The letter is structured as a collage. The first sentence un-scrolls in a short Audenian mixture of two and three beat lines that culminate in a question:

Sex fingers toes
in the marketplace
near your father's church
in Hamlet, North Carolina —
witness to this love
in this calm fallow
of these minds,
there is no substitute for pain:
genitals gone or going,
seed burned out,
you tuck the roots in the earth,
turn back, and move
by river through the swamps,
singing: *a love supreme, a love*
   supreme;
what does it all mean?

I never fully understood the harsh but cryptic first two lines until I read an interview in which Harper said that the first three words are the genitals, fingers,

and toes of Sam Hose, who was brutally lynched, butchered, and burned alive by a white mob in Coweta County, Georgia, in 1899. Harper seems to be taking the racist spectacle of a lynching, linking it back to the slave trade, and anachronistically relocating it near the church in the North Carolina town where Coltrane was born in 1926. The narrator thus proceeds to tell Coltrane's story — the tenor sax seems to be playing *A Love Supreme* while he is dying — inflected by a historical Black martyrdom.

I'm struck by the way the intimate tone ("Dear John") jostles and even contends with the symbolic meaning ("Dear Coltrane"). It's almost as if Harper reaches back to Egyptian mythology, an African antecedent, for the story of the death and resurrection of Osiris, which licenses him to treat Coltrane as a scapegoat figure, a dying and reviving god, a king whose seed is buried so that it can be regenerated. The musician heads to the urban North, to "the electric city" — probably Philadelphia, where Coltrane started to make his true music, to transform the sorrow of the blues with a new passion and intensity: "You pick up the horn / with some will and blow / into the freezing night: / *a love supreme, a love supreme.*"

The first two stanzas are presented in an ongoing present tense: "Dawn comes and you cook / up the thick sin…" Stanza two addresses Coltrane's heroin addiction, the space he inhabited "between impotence and death," the terrible need that fuels "the tenor sax cannibal." It condenses into seven lines Coltrane's long struggle to get clean, to find independence. The section ends with the refrain line, the fourth time that Harper repeats "*a love supreme.*" He is imitating Coltrane and wringing the changes out of the phrase.

Narumi Nekpenekpen, *double dutch cherry chaser, star licker*, 2020. Courtesy the artist and Deli Gallery, NY.

Coltrane grew up in a religious environment — his father preached, and both of his grandfathers were ministers — and became deeply religious as he overcame his addiction. That's why the third italicized stanza cuts to the call and response of a Black Pentecostal church. Listen to it again and you feel almost as if you're participating in a service:

Why you so black?
cause I am
why you so funky?
cause I am
why you so black?
cause I am
why you so sweet?
cause I am
why you so black?
cause I am
a love supreme, a love supreme:

This is the most vernacular part of the poem ("*why you so funky?*") and links the preacher to the parishioners, the musician to the community. The tone is lighter than elsewhere in the poem, but the meaning is serious, a pointed rhetorical interrogation of Blackness. Every question culminates in the same determined, existential answer: "*cause I am.*" Yet the enjambment in the last two lines cleverly brings the questioning to a larger conclusion: "*cause I am / a love supreme, a love supreme.*" Harper views Coltrane, as he would view Hayden, as a figure of transcendence.

The church section ends with a colon, not a period, and turns the supreme love downward to Coltrane's earthly struggle with addiction. The last stanza moves as one sentence across 12 lines. The liftoff is remarkable. The speaker reenters the poem as a communal "we," a stand-in for the community, as in a ballad. The repetitions enact the intensities:

So sick
you couldn't play *Naima,*
so flat we ached
for song you'd concealed
with your own blood,
your diseased liver gave
out its purity,
the inflated heart
pumps out, the tenor kiss,
tenor love:
a love supreme, a love supreme —
a love supreme, a love supreme —

Harper inaugurates the last movement by recalling a time when Coltrane was too sick to play his signature ballad, "Naima," and contrasts the musician's diseased body, his physical sacrifice, his martyrdom, with the pure music that he attains, what "the inflated heart / pumps out." The two elements of the poem, the intimate address to "Dear John" and the symbolic address to "Dear Coltrane," come together and reach a high rhetorical pitch. The erotic charge and progression — "the tenor kiss, / tenor love" — reaches its culmination in the final transcendent repetition of the refrain: "*a love supreme, a love supreme — / a love supreme, a love supreme — .*"

"Dear John, Dear Coltrane" ends with a dash and not a period, as if to suggest that the poem is open-ended, the ending interrupted, indeterminate. This indicates that Coltrane's idea of a supreme love is ongoing and continuous, an unceasing legacy. But the strong repetitive chant at the end also takes us back to the beginning and brings the poem full cycle. It has the ritual closure of a valedictory epistle, a letter of farewell. Harper found it difficult, maybe even impossible, to accept that he had written an elegy for John Coltrane even before Coltrane had died. Orpheus was gone, but he had left behind his music, which Michael Harper, his poetic protégé, would go on listening to and imitating, disheartened and enraged by social injustice but also continuing to seek transcendence, writing historical indictments but also love letters and elegies, homages and hymns.

THE WASH

NATALIA REYES

Mirna shielded her face with the bill of her visor, guarding against the quicksilver of light-reflecting roofs. She made time through the neighborhood toward the brown mountains in the west, beyond the mirages of heat. Candy, as usual, lagged. It was hard for her, with the weight of 13 years, the grumbling. At the edge of town, the crags towered over the municipal nature preserve. Quail Trail, named for its coveys of native birds, was delightful, Mirna's favorite. It embraced the lip of the enormous concrete wash that collected flash floods in freak weather, curving through a landscape of smoke trees and creosote. In the winter, sultry petrichor followed light rains. In spring, the wildflowers bloomed among the cholla cacti, and mother quails led their young, warbling with top knots bobbing, away from danger. There was no autumn.

Summers, of course, were brutal. It was especially bad for Mirna, who went door to door hawking cookware for commission, dressed in slacks and a button-up that registered her sweat as easily as she imagined her voice registered her need. The job, with its uncertainty and its slammed doors and its hours of selling on foot, made it much less appealing to spend her days off exercising with Candy through infernal heat. It didn't help that she made these walks hard on Mirna, her complaints relentless as the sun. The warmth, the dust, the bugs, the sweat, the senselessness — Candy hated all of it.

There was no use arguing with her. Candy had a response ready for almost anything Mirna could say. It had been hard enough to get her to agree to the exercise when they began two months ago. Candy had come this close — she had held her index finger and thumb half an inch apart — to running away when Mirna announced her egregiously ambitious plan of weekly speed-walking. Mirna had not known what "egregiously" meant but had laughed anyway.

"How would you run away?" she had asked. "You can barely walk." It had been one of the few times she had no rebuttal. In the end, she had agreed. It had helped to have Dr. Cariño prescribe the physical activity. Candy, despite her rudeness and her distrust and her perfect knowledge, respected science and medicine, or what she understood of it, anyway. Yes, she'd go on these walks. Yes, she'd follow Mirna. But she wouldn't like it. And with every puff and strain and groan, Candy made her feelings clear.

As she approached the dune that marked the entrance to the trail, Mirna stopped, waiting for her daughter. She was a block behind, seeming to drag her body across the earth. When she reached her mother, her face was red. Sweat beaded on the fuzz of her upper lip.

"Why did I agree to this?" she asked in a mumble.

"I told you," Mirna said. "Dr. Cariño said you're pre-diabetic. You have to lose some of that fat. Oh, how I wish you'd put on sunscreen, you're dark as it is." She took the visor from her head and tried to place it on her daughter's head, but Candy dodged her.

"Just think about how much better you'll look if we keep at it," Mirna said. The elastic waistband of Candy's gym shorts strained against her stomach, and the hems stretched on the width of her thighs. The mottled gray and white of her shirt rippled as she inhaled and exhaled. Mirna had never been so large as a child. In fact, she had been thin, underfed — malnourished. She didn't know what to blame for her daughter's weight. Sometimes she thought it was this country's foods, so unlike the ones she had known growing up. Other times she thought maybe she was to blame, that somehow, in feeding her daughter, she had done something wrong.

"I don't get what the problem is," Candy said. "I'm fat, so I'm ugly? Dr. Cariño's as fat as they come, and I don't see her sweating it out like this."

Mirna shook her head.

"So it's not about the pre-diabetes? It's that I'm ugly? You might as well tell the truth."

Mirna did not reply. It wasn't that her daughter was ugly. She just wasn't pretty, and not because she couldn't be. Mirna tried to prove to her that she was ready to do what it took — waxing, trimming, makeup, exercise — to help her feel better about herself. But except for the walks, Candy refused. Beauty was a multibillion-dollar industry bent on making girls hate themselves, she said, to which Mirna usually said nothing. Mirna thought that people only bought what was useful, what made sense. Clearly, women around the world needed the products. It was one of the things she believed about Royal Prestige; people wouldn't buy her wares if the grease-burning quality of the metal were just a sales pitch. It was frustrating that Mirna's low-fat Royal Prestige meals did nothing for Candy, who only grew bigger and bigger each year. And Candy would not grant herself the minor relief of cosmetic help. That she insisted on her non-beauty was most frustrating of all.

This didn't stop Mirna from expecting things of Candy. She had named her after the protagonist in *Candy Candy*, an anime Mirna had watched in Spanish that was, hands down, the best show on television when Mirna was a girl. The Candy in the show was blonde and kind, adventurous and brave. Before Candy had been born, Mirna had imagined the years they would spend together, the fun they would have. It was the mindset of a young, naïve mother, she now knew, and nothing had worked out quite as expected. She had, for instance, thought that her child would look with wonder out at the world. She had believed, foolishly, that children came into life impervious to its harms, and that raising them was as easy as raising the goats she had bottle-fed as a girl. It was a matter of habits, of feeding and burping and washing and clothing, of cooing and bouncing them on the knee. But time taught her that it was more difficult than that. It was colic and fever and vomit and shit. And Candy wasn't a happy child.

She was uneasy, wide-eyed and afraid as a toddler, cockatiel nervous as she entered school. In the last few years, she had become sullen and cynical and much too smart. She spoke in words that reminded Mirna how little she knew, and this unsettled her. Only when she brought excellent marks home did Mirna think this a good thing. If she was so smart at so young an age, how much smarter would she become with time? Mirna rubbed her thighs absentmindedly, feeling the skin he had made tender beneath the cloth. Candy had something Mirna didn't. And maybe, just maybe, it would spare her daughter her fate.

"Up the hill," Mirna instructed. "Let's pick flowers." She hopped her nimble feet up the sandy incline. She could feel the stagnant blood in her legs as she climbed. Her daughter groaned and followed.

They often picked flowers on their morning walks, though sometimes they collected stones. The flowers were better, in part, because all the stones were the same — chunks of granite, brittle and banal — but the flowers were all special, Mirna felt, given how hardy they must be to survive. The flowers were good, too, because they required more effort to pick. This was the real purpose of her game. She had Candy pick flowers to incorporate stretching and kneeling into their walks, hoping all the squatting would induce that muscle tone Dr. Cariño so wanted. At first, Candy had resisted Mirna's game. She had called it idiotic, kicked a boulder, stubbed her toe. Mirna had pointed out that flowers couldn't hurt her.

Today, Candy seemed relieved to pick flowers, or so Mirna thought. The sun beat down with insistence, and she couldn't keep a quick pace. The flowers — sand verbena, tamarisk, desert lavender — gave her an excuse to rest. If she knelt by the spindly scrub for purple buds or stretched into the branches of a desert willow for delicate orchid blooms, Mirna allowed her some stillness, some peace. She made a great show of it at first. She sighed and blew a raspberry so that sweat flew out in all directions. Then, she knelt, right hand on her wide lower back, knees extending past her ankles, her eyes on her mother's. When she dislodged a blossom from a tiny bush — "Careful with the needles!" Mirna said — she made certain Mirna was looking in her eyes, so she could roll them like tumbleweeds.

"Nicely done," Mirna said. Dr. Cariño had recommended praise.

"It's just a dumb flower," Candy said. She crushed the blossom in her palm.

Mirna bristled but tried to ignore it. She could enjoy these walks if she coaxed herself into the right mindset. She persuaded herself into gratitude to her past self for designing this game weeks ago, as picking flowers proved more pleasant than the walk. In the shade of palo verde trees, she could almost forget the heat. Her sweat was wicking and cool. She settled near a spiny menodora from where she could watch Candy, who picked up a short, knobby stick, the arm of a smoke tree, and with it bent willow branches and inspected shrubs for stinkbugs. If a bush was clear of the angular insects, she knelt and picked, not just flowers (for the midsummer made them scarce), but coils of white bursage, sprigs of black greasewood, tufts of saltbush. The hot soil released its scent into the air. The flowers and branches swayed in Candy's arms. Mirna felt keen, nearly light, her body tired and her mind near clear. Her daughter, occupied

with the brambles of a creosote bush, paid her no mind.

When Mirna approached such tranquility, something inside her trembled, precarious at the prospect of peace. She felt it now, that familiar wariness. The western mountains enclosed her despite the wide desert, and she remembered her hometown, its rushing rivers, its mournful ghosts, in that country to the south. It had not afforded her a moment of rest. She had kept moving then, rushing from corn mill to market to corral, afraid of what would happen if she stopped. It was how she'd crossed to this side, how she'd come to live here. It was how she now sold pots and pans. In the evenings, she flitted around the kitchen like a restless bird, making dinner before he arrived because if it wasn't as hot as he liked it and already served, it would end up in the trash if she was lucky, on her if she was not. She believed in moving, did not still even at night, her teeth grinding. To approach such peace in the desert dust made her anxious; it reminded her of death. She felt her coagulated blood. She could not stand it. She wanted to run. Mirna rose to her feet.

"Start running," Mirna said. She began to jog in place.

"But why?" Candy asked, looking over her shoulder at her mother. "We just started picking. I haven't even collected that many. Look." She pivoted on her heels with a grunt, still squatting, and held out her arms to her mother. Coils of quailbush spilled from them, and the fuzzy tips of creosote branches drifted to the ground like dandelion puffs.

"We have to get your heart rate up." She could tell Candy was considering it from the way she twisted her lips and squinted at her.

"But I thought you wanted me to tone."

"You have to do both. It's like circuit training."

Candy drew up the corner of her mouth. She sensed the lie, Mirna could tell. She knew she had lost her when she pulled her arms close again, crushing the petals and leaves, and pivoted with another grunt back to the bush she'd been inspecting.

"In P.E., my teacher told us not to run between the hours of ten and four. She said it could cause heat stroke."

Mirna slowed her jog and stopped. In her mottled gray shirt, hunched over and squatting like that, her wide back to her, Candy resembled a boulder. She looked like a boulder perched on the two smaller rocks of her legs, the calves thick and round. Mirna let her gaze blur and looked at her stone of a child. With her gaze not quite right, Candy looked even more like a chunk of mountain, her brown ponytail a stripe of dark mineral, her body seismically shuddering from her girth and from the heat waves which made fata morganas of everything, even slabs of girl. Her daughter was infrequently the person she wanted her to be, and it seemed like another injustice in the slew of injustices that formed her life. If not peace, she deserved some relief, some release. So what if the P.E. teacher said running in the sun could cause heat stroke? Mirna knew for a fact the P.E. teacher was a chain-smoker. She saw her sucking on tar at morning drop-off every day, killing herself slowly only to turn around and teach her child the mechanics of health. No, Mirna couldn't stand such hypocrisy. Not with this heat. Not when her body quivered so. She felt

her skin throb beneath the synthetic fibers of her shorts. She let her eyes rest.

"You're young. Young people don't get heat stroke."

"Wrong," Candy said. Her hair bobbed above her shoulders as she shook her head. "People of any age can get heat stroke. The substitute said so in Health."

So now she was competing with a substitute, a person Candy knew for one hour of her life. Mirna wished she could run on her own. She wished she was not saddled with the burden of whittling Candy down until she became a different person. The task fell to her because, of course, her father would have nothing to do with it. He only belittled her, calling her fatty every night. It was too hard, too hot for this. The oppressive rays scorched her and reflected upon the bleached sand below. The sand's reflection burned, too. She felt pressurized, tinned, the dry air of her barren surroundings like a vacuum into which any sound she made — any bit of spit — might vaporize and sizzle into irrelevance. It was difficult to think. Candy was stubborn, and the heat was not helping. She took one step, then two, and then she was right behind Candy. She towered over her crouched form and tapped her on the shoulder.

"Tag, you're it!" Mirna said. She jogged backward away from her daughter, waiting for her to stand.

Candy tossed her stick to the ground and gathered her flowers, clutching them tight in her fist, and heaved her body up, a ripple moving through her. She turned to follow Mirna, and Mirna saw something in her face that made her slow, almost stop. It wasn't the defiance Mirna had expected to see. Instead, it was pure effort, distilled exertion marred by something else, resignation or defeat. Her brows were set. Her

Kayla Ephros, *clouds*, 2020, graphite on paper, 8.5 x 11 inches. Courtesy of the artist.

eyes looked fatigued. It was the depth of them that made Mirna trip a little. They had always been deep-set, Candy's eyes, hazel like her father's. The thin, veined skin beneath the sockets was purplish, lending gravity to her face since infancy, from the first moment Mirna had seen her. She had weighed six pounds and four ounces, the skin underneath the smear of vernix violet like a bruise. Candy had almost choked inside Mirna's womb, wrapped as her neck was in the umbilical cord. She emerged a shade of indigo and so quiet, Mirna thought her stillborn. Mirna had begun to cry before anyone could tell her the child was alive, a shudder that left no room for breathing or thought. She had blamed herself. She had allowed him to hit her while the baby was growing, and this was the result. When Candy finally squirmed in her arms, her eyes squeezing tight and then opening wide as she gasped for breath, Mirna saw the depth in them, like two wells into which she could disappear. And that's what she had tried to do for a time — disappear into that little body, feed it and care for it as if it might sustain her through life's blows. But not in years. In fact, she avoided looking at her daughter as much as she could. When the other two had flushed out of her, drowned in the porcelain bowl, Mirna had shut her eyes against them, her chest flooded with relief, and that was the start of no longer seeing. As Candy stood, her body shuddering with every step, the bouquet in her fist buffeted by the air, Mirna couldn't avoid her. And though the morning and the weeks and the months had been occupied with making Candy less, making her small, the years Mirna spent raising her loomed suddenly large, like the mountain peaks in the distance. Mirna turned away.

"Catch me," she said. She began to run.

The desert lay before her like an immense sieve shimmering in the heat and, as Mirna ran, she imagined dissolving through it. The gravel and pebbles and sand crunched beneath her. She imagined falling through the rocks like a pillar of dust. As she swung her arms forward and back, her momentum grew, and she sped up and thought she might disappear faster until she was nothing. Her bruises prickled, and her shaking thighs made her eyes water until she couldn't tell if her eyelashes caught the salt of her sweat or her tears. It was hard to see. The sun rose and rose, and with it the temperature, and Mirna was at the edge of the wash — a vast valley in the mountain cove, a dry lakebed for flash floods — before she even thought to look back.

But she did. She turned around and jogged backward, her hands balled up into bobbing fists. She expected to see Candy, slow and far but there, behind her. Instead, she saw only the broad, speckled desert, soil tinged gray, shining white in the raging sun, and not a Candy — not close, not far, not anywhere — in sight.

Mirna stopped, her arms dropping, the hands now loose. It was not unusual for her to go too far. She had devised this challenge as a real game, truly fun — as a girl, she had loved tag. The original objective had been for mother and daughter to take turns catching each other among the cacti. Mirna's great oversight had become quickly apparent: Candy was simply too slow. She struggled to navigate around the low desert scrub and became paralyzed at the sight of stinkbugs. She wasted breath and energy lamenting, as if in religious chant, how much she *hated* tag. The only time Mirna had simply let Candy tag her, she had deflated like a pricked balloon. The wattle of her second chin had rested on the plane of her chest with a dejection so complete that Mirna had ached to scoop Candy into her arms and carry her home. Since that day, Mirna had conceded a change to the rules: she need only follow her mother at her own pace without needing to tag Mirna. The caveat was that she must not stop until she did reach her mother, wherever her mother may be.

It was this last expectation that propelled Mirna to retrace her steps. To keep running wasn't so much to ask. Candy had one responsibility, and that was to try. Mirna imagined her sitting on a boulder in the shade of a tree, inspecting her wilted bouquet. Her overworked heart would beat fast, the cramp in her side a reminder of the muscles hidden deep. Her sweat would cool her while Mirna burned in the sun. There she was, her daughter's gullible fool. She could be a selfish child, concerned only with her comfort, ready to treat Mirna like an idiot who couldn't think. It was maddening. She was just like her father. This thought only made her run faster. She felt like hitting something.

Mirna ran until she was back where she started, in the gathering of palo verdes and smoke trees where she'd left Candy. The girl was not there. She seemed to be nowhere. For a moment, Mirna couldn't see. Everything was a negative of itself. She registered only the keening whistle of a military jet flying overhead, saw its long contrail across the empty sky. If she had walked herself home, Mirna didn't know what she would do. She was beyond the age Mirna could tell her father to punish her, to beat her as he had when she couldn't wrap her mind around the

concept of a training toilet and squatted on the living room floor. It was sometimes the only way she would learn. She had been stubborn. She was stubborn still. That was the problem.

When Mirna opened the door to Candy's bedroom, she discovered she was not there, and a quick search through all the rooms in the house, including the garage, showed she had not set foot there since first walking out into the day's light. Her belongings were still there, nothing tossed about, no missing bag. Everything was just as before, all things in their proper place. Except for Candy, whose proper place seemed to be now, to Mirna, right beside her.

Mirna looked for Candy along the path. She felt ridiculous to be looking in the desert when what she'd always liked about it, the reason she felt safe leaving her behind, was how few places there were in it to hide. With Candy lost, every inclination of the land, every dense clump of barrel cactus and cholla felt like an invitation for her to secret herself away.

But she hadn't been anywhere she could think to find her. She wasn't by the cairns on the trailhead to the steep rock face where seasoned climbers tested their mettle on crumbling slate. She wasn't near the maze lined with rocks like Nazca lines. She wasn't huddled in the shade of the concrete reservoir, graffiti-tagged and long since emptied. There was no sign of her by the rest stop with the water fountains and benches, no sign of her by the coyote caves. Mirna climbed to the top of an outcropping of rock and forced her gaze across the whiteness of the land, the brightness making her squint. She was looking for a body among the boulders, but either the gray of Candy's shirt blended into the sand or it didn't exist.

She reached the base of the mountain. She could spend hours walking the barrens of rock and still come upon nothing. Hikers went into these mountains and didn't come back. They appeared in the news, photos of fit men and women with all the proper gear lost to the sand and heat. Who might she call? She now regretted refusing her daughter a cell phone. She certainly couldn't call him. He didn't like being disturbed at work and, besides, it would only make him angry. Once, while packing the groceries into the car when Candy was a year old, she'd left the keys inside and had forgotten to leave one door open. The car had automatically locked. It was a hot day like this one, and she had pleaded at Candy's door, pointing at the lock, which was within reach of her daughter's tiny fist. But she was too young to understand, patting her hands against the window, and Mirna too frightened at her mistake, too overwhelmed. She had called him. When he had arrived, his face more furrowed than usual, he had pushed her aside, a household iron in his hand. He used it to heat the acrylic backing of carpet to affix it to tack strip in flooring installations, but on that day with Candy locked inside, he had swung his arm back and beat it against the window. The glass had resisted at first, but then it gave, shattering into hundreds of pieces all over Candy, who had the good instinct to cover her face. He was too furious to think clearly and had pulled her through the window, scratching her thighs against the jagged glass. It was only then that the baby had cried.

As Mirna came upon a tangle of tumbleweeds gathered at the base of the mountain, she thought of her daughter that day. There was a song about a little frog's tail that Mirna sang whenever something ailed her baby, and she had sung it to her, rubbing the scratches on her thighs. But just as Mirna had calmed her down, her father had started to yell, and Mirna was humiliated in plain public sight. Candy had not remained calm. She had started to cry, had not stopped for hours, and Mirna merely held her. It was only in the warm water of the bath that Candy had stopped, her little chest heaving in that way that chests do when a body's all cried out.

It was then that Mirna remembered the oasis. Through a pass in the mountain, and then a narrow path that crept along its edge, past a valley and a downhill slope so steep one had to use one's hands to descend, there existed a palm oasis, a huddle of fronds and grasses. A natural spring bubbled up from the aquifer. Mirna and Candy had chanced upon it two years ago, when Candy's energy had been higher, her heart not as hard. It was a place they both enjoyed, a rare bit of water on the arid land, and it felt like a secret only they knew about. Once, Mirna had packed sandwiches and snacks, and they'd made a picnic of it, Candy sunning herself on a flat rock, her toes dipping into the water. It was clear, so clear Mirna suspected one could drink from it, and she had remembered the river in her hometown, the white froth of the rapids, how she would cup her hands and sip. Remembering the river, the oasis, Candy's wide face, she sped up. Her fear was irrational, imprecise. She could only tether it to the image of her daughter's face like a specter, a face not of this world.

She reached the oasis, her hands covered in dust from inching down the incline. She might see her as she had at age

11, warming herself on the rock. She had taken to the heat like a salamander then, but no longer. She didn't see her along the rim of the water, and she started looking through the scrub beneath the palms. Mirna's desperation had reached a fine point and she realized the rivulets streaming down her face were not of sweat, but tears. She was crying. As she realized this, she started to shout.

"Candy!" she yelled. "Candy! Where are you?"

Her voice did not travel far. She shouted Candy's name until her mouth was dry and she couldn't form words. Sounds bubbled forth. She could not understand herself, could not decipher her noise. This was her fault. Candy was gone, and it was her doing. She sat on the rock by the water. Her daughter was right. Dr. Cariño was as fat as they came, and what did it matter? She was a doctor. She didn't sell pots and pans in the damned heat. She didn't tack carpet with a house iron. She ate. And isn't that what they wanted, anyway, when it came down to it? Isn't that why they had trekked across the desert to this infernal country, their hearts frenetic in their too-thin chests beneath cover of night? At least in their town, they hadn't walked in the blazing sun. At least there, they hadn't burned like this.

The water bubbled. Mirna stilled. Had she imagined it? She leapt up and looked. The pond was moving, the surface breaking. Mirna put palms to mouth to quiet herself. A ghostly face rippled the surface, round like the moon, waxen and frightful. It was a face she had seen before, 13 years ago, a face with pinched eyelids and a pinched mouth, the life gone out of it. An old fear filled her. She felt it down into the gummed plasma beneath her skin. But the fear was not a 13-year-old fear. It was

a younger fear, the fear that had rankled her in all the months leading up to the moment her not-yet babies had flushed out of her into the porcelain bowl. It was not that the waxen face in the water was dead. It was that, against Mirna's will, it was alive. It was alive and, in a few moments, it would be gasping for breath, for teat, and Mirna would be stuck with him just as before, dependent on him to satisfy the living face's insatiable hunger, its spite.

Mirna ran into the water. In the center, it was deep. She sank, her shoes gripped by silt. The bottom held tight, and she went under. Her kicking muddied the spring. The dirt glinted, struck by shafts of light. Her daughter's face was white and grinning. Her eyes were closed. Mirna reached out and placed her hands on Candy's shoulders, on either side of her neck. How easy it would be, how simple, to take her neck in her hands and wring until the life drained out of her. How wonderful, to be released from the burden of love. To walk in the desert when she wanted rather than because she must, to have what she desired because there wasn't another life siphoning it all away, a smart and disobedient and ungrateful thing. How easy, to do away with the years of mistakes she could not look in the eyes — how right.

But Mirna could not bring her hands to her daughter's neck. The violet gravity of those closed eyes stopped her. She felt her arms tense with the contradiction of her desire, her wish to be free of it all. Then her muscles relaxed. She slid her hands down to her daughter's waist and held her. Candy opened her eyes. They were deep-set and hazel, just like his. Mirna would know those eyes for the rest of her days. She took her daughter in her arms and pushed toward the light.

THE LADY IN THE TENT

KRISTEN BROWNELL

I.

I'm in line at the Brentwood farmer's market waiting to buy organic kale and avocados (I realize at this moment that I've become one of *those* people) when I see her.

Most people don't acknowledge the woman holding the sign, or her army-style utility tent — it has just enough room to lie on your belly and escape from the elements, like a soldier in the battlefield — nestled between two overgrown rose bushes. It's spring and the bushes are starting to sprout pink roses, perky and beautiful, their petals open and ready for their coming-out party. But most people in this neighborhood don't acknowledge the flowers, either — they're too busy talking on the phone, packing their trunk with overpriced food, making happy hour plans, heading off to pick up their kids from private school. The life concerns of folks in a neighborhood like this.

When it's my turn to pay, I throw in an apple, a bag of cashews, and an Evian. My car is parked near the lady in the tent. I assume her sign has something to do with food, and I prepare to hand her the apple, nuts, and water. But I'm wrong. Her sign doesn't request food, or work, or even money. I squint to get a better look:

MENSTRUAL PRODUCTS, PLEASE.

I pause and mentally review what's in my purse. Like most women, I have a secret compartment with a stash of tampons, feminine wipes, and Midol. I say hello, and hand her the stash. She thanks me, her face morphing from concern to relief, though she won't make eye contact. I give her the food and water.

"If I'd known, I would've gotten you some chocolate," I joke. She smiles and finally meets my gaze. A woman pushing a dog stroller walks by and watches us disapprovingly; she reads the homeless woman's sign but chooses to ignore it, like so many others before her.

"What's your name?" I ask.

She hesitates. "They call me Missy." She says her name as if it's not hers, and I imagine it probably isn't.

Missy's eyes drop to my purse, which is one of those ridiculous and rather poorly made designer handbags, and I'm embarrassed by my materialism. Her eyes shift to Dog Stroller Lady, who's still glaring at us. Missy thanks me again, says goodbye, and quickly disappears into her tent.

I drive off and try to go about my day, but I'm unable to stop thinking about Missy. And it's not because she's homeless — the homeless population in Los Angeles is staggering, and tent encampments have become commonplace — it's because she's a homeless *woman*, alone. She doesn't know it, but I understand how she feels and what she's going through more than she will ever know, or ever believe. When I was homeless, I never thought to ask for menstrual products, though truth be told it's one of the worst aspects of being an unsheltered woman.

I see a Target and impulsively pull into the parking lot. Thirty minutes later I leave with several bags of feminine products and provisions, including some Dove chocolate, and a couple packs of underwear and socks — the most requested items in homeless shelters are underwear and socks. I go back to the shrubs, armed with the care package.

It's too late — Missy is gone.

II.

It's a fact that an overwhelming number of homeless women end up that way because they've suffered some form of abuse. The women I knew when I was on the streets were there for that reason, and I was there for that reason, too. It wasn't just that I'd suffered a disturbing amount of abuse — it was that I was desperate to escape it. I was willing to walk away from everything, even the basics of human survival, to escape it.

I should've seen it coming, but I didn't. Or maybe I did but didn't want to believe it would come to pass — after all, he did have one of the worst tempers and shortest fuses I've ever witnessed. But I was 18 years old, it was my first serious relationship, and I was so determined to show my family that dropping out of high school and running away to Las Vegas to be with a man I'd met just once before in a casino bar (as you do) wasn't a bad idea. I was willing to put up with anything to prove I hadn't made an epic mistake.

Five years later when I found myself living in my car (and sometimes a tent) near Fremont Street, I formed a group with several other homeless women who roamed the area — we called ourselves the Woe Luck Club (you will never find a person with a better sense of humor than a homeless person). Some of them were exotic dancers at the Glitter Gulch or, like me, they simply scavenged to survive. We would share liquor and stories of how we ended up there, and our "first times" — first time dumpster diving, first time asking a stranger for money, first time coming up with an innovative way to deal with our periods without proper products, first time darting through a casino draining discarded cocktail glasses until security eighty-sixed us. Then we'd laugh at our shenanigans, like a pack of neighborhood kids who'd just been told to get off the neighbor's lawn.

We also shared stories of our first time being abused. For many of us, it was the first time — another first time — we'd verbalized the experience. Mine was when he was trying to teach me how to use a stick shift. After a disaster of a driving lesson, we went home and he threw a suitcase at my back. I felt silly when I told the girls this, because it seemed so tame compared to some of their first times. It wasn't that there was a "best stories" competition, or that we were trying to one-up each other. But some of them had been scarred, even disfigured — one of the girls had been

shot in the face and you could still see the evidence on her cheek — right off the bat during that first time, and those were just the wounds you could physically see.

Almost every single one of us had developed a drug or alcohol problem as a result of the abuse we'd suffered. For many of us, that abuse had gone on for years. By the time I ended up calling my Honda hatchback home, I had experienced other kinds of abuse outside of the relationship I was in from men I worked for, men I worked with, men I considered to be friends, men who came to performances, "normal" men, strange men, random men. The funny thing is that in many ways I felt safer living in the underbelly than I had living in the real world — here, it was easier to hide, to be invisible, to disguise myself as a man, to achieve a level of unattractiveness that would deter any man from ever violating me again. What I didn't realize at the time is that abuse isn't about sex — it's about power, and control.

Though I had nothing to my name, those were two things I finally felt like I had over my own life.

III.

Like Missy (I suspect), the girls and I all had a "street name." I chose "Cleo," because in better times I'd played Cleopatra at Caesars Palace. The homeless rarely share their real names unless they absolutely have to. It helps you separate yourself from your real identity, like this isn't really *you*. No — this is simply a role you're playing, much like the queen of the Nile and all the other roles I'd played during my time as a showgirl. The street is a stage of a different sort, but a stage all the same.

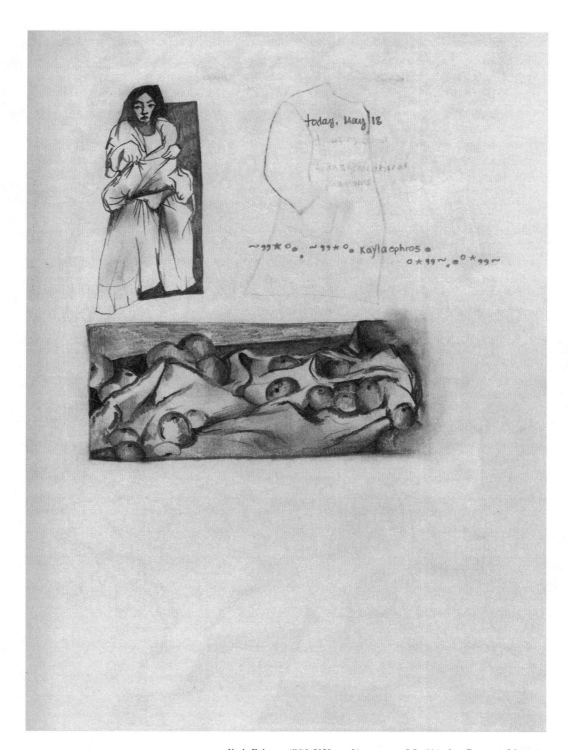

Kayla Ephros, *still life*, 2020, graphite on paper, 8.5 x 11 inches. Courtesy of the artist.

Looking back, I'd been role-playing long before I arrived in Vegas. This is true of many girls like me, including my Woe Luck Club sisters, who were raised in the 1980s on Disney princess movies and fairy-tale culture; this was long before Tiana, Merida, and Mulan. Like so many of my friends, my dad's nickname for me growing up was "Princess." I was brought up to believe that women should be docile, demure, feminine, slender, clean, smiling, uncomplaining, nice-smelling, well mannered, put together, a slave to pink and purple, and, of course, beautiful. And if you weren't all of these things at all times, well, then, shame on you!

As a teen, I remember hearing one of my dad's friends say once that, "Women should poop in packets." I pictured someone scrambling around to pick up after me like a dog-walker with compostable bags and a pooper-scooper. I learned from a young age that burping like my uncles, farting like my brothers, or having a *Dumb and Dumber* moment in the bathroom was something I and every other woman was forbidden to do.

When I started working as a model for a Las Vegas talent agency at age 18 and later as a performer, it seemed that this princess had, after a rather long period in adolescence as the homely and awkward Cinderella stepsister, started to blossom into Cinderella herself. At first, I loved the attention, loved being paraded around, loved being the embodiment of female "perfection"; I loved all the potential princes (and, in fact, I actually dated Prince for a time) hovering around wanting to "court" me.

The fairy tale eventually became a cautionary one.

When I found myself homeless — when I was no longer any of those things I'd been raised to be — the failure I felt as a woman was remarkable. *I now have to defecate in public* — could I even still call myself a woman? The conflict between wanting to make myself unattractive because of what I'd been through and mourning my former hyper-femininity occupied my thoughts almost as much as figuring out what I needed to do to survive the day. I was supposed to be a damsel, after all; I was supposed to be the lady in the tower waiting for a man to come and rescue me.

No one ever told me what to do if I ended up the lady in the tent instead.

IV.

In the end, it wasn't a man, or anyone else who rescued me from the tent. In the end, I had to rescue myself.

I was lucky, because I had a family to turn to, particularly my mother, who, once I was ready to get help, took me in no questions asked. She didn't know the extent of how low I'd been, and she sensed not to ask. Until recently, no one knew. I honestly believed that being homeless was a period of my life I'd never speak of, ever. Women are pressured, even bullied, to take so many painful secrets to the grave, and I thought this would be another one of mine.

Many years have passed since I was on the streets, but that failure I felt — not just as a woman, but as a human being — is still very much alive in me. Our culture has been conditioned to interpret and portray such life events as a failure. *Your alcoholism and bad decision-making is what landed you there — don't blame it on anyone else!* It's true that I and everyone else in the world should take responsibility for the choices we make — I truly believe that. But in reality, the situation is much more layered than that, and goes well beyond the scope of an essay. Every homeless situation does. Many unsheltered individuals don't have a choice, or feel they don't have one, or can't make one.

Homelessness is one of the number one crises this country faces, and the pandemic has underscored the reality that life on the streets is often just one (small) decision or disaster away. It can happen to anyone, at any moment. It can happen to the person you least suspect. You probably know someone who has once been or is currently homeless and don't realize it, because to admit it is to face criticism, incredulity, shame, gossip, pity. Historically, homelessness has been discussed in a way that focuses on the homeless themselves as the root of the problem, that they "messed up" to such a degree that losing everything was inevitable, even deserved.

The lack of empathy I see, hear, and feel when the national conversation turns to homelessness is unnerving, as is the lack of direct voice the homeless and formerly homeless are given. Yet so many believe they have the authority and knowledge to speak on our behalf. It's one thing to look at numbers and statistics and costs, and to focus on the "inconvenience" of people like Missy. It's quite another to imagine the people and human experiences and suffering behind these numbers.

Women are especially vulnerable. We're paid less and promoted less; it's more difficult for us to get ahead, especially single mothers. We're the biggest targets and victims of abuse, rape, violence, crime, and murder, particularly poor women, homeless women, and women of color. At the same time, the burden on women to "hold it together" and to "be a

lady" at all times is enormous. The diversity of pressures we face is astounding, and the lack of support and resources we often face is, too.

I still think about the members of the Woe Luck Club and wonder what happened to them. By the time I left Las Vegas in 2005 and moved back to my hometown of Los Angeles, most of the group had scattered. Some of the girls went to shelters. Some, like me, were able to get help from family. We were able to begin again, to go to college, to become a teacher, to pursue a PhD. Education is what saved me, and has made me feel like a true "princess."

Like Missy, some of the girls — too many of them — vanished. When I think about them, I remember them as real women, as human beings with histories and feelings and desires and dreams, not just ladies in tents. These women are daughters, mothers, wives, aunts, friends. These women are your fellow citizens, your neighbors. These women are you.

Please stop ignoring the signs.

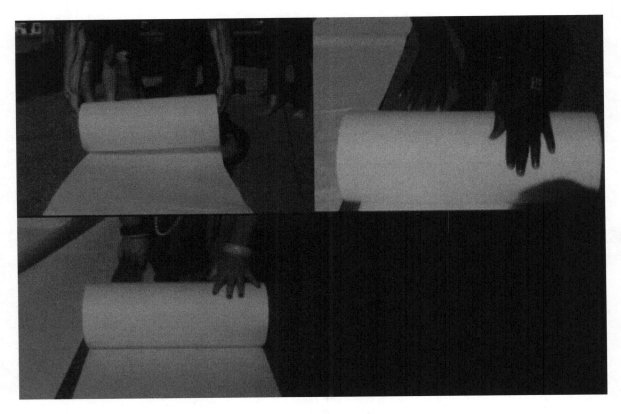

Brontez Purnell, still from *Free Jazz*, 2013, 8 mm film. Performed by Brontez Purnell Dance Company.

"So it's a common misconception that the title of this work is a statement on Jazz music (as most of the music in the movie is not Jazz music at all). 'Free Jazz' as a title is a statement on Jazz dance. I remember reading an outdated book about Jazz dance in College (the name escapes me) but it mentioned the fact that the original 'Jazz' musicians rejected the word Jazz at first at it was a media invention and not what they themselves had termed it at all. I was obsessed with the idea or the notion that on a performing black body all movement becomes 'Jazz' of sorts. (I was a quite a party kid back in my day and would notice that every five years whatever new black dance that entered the mainstream eye was then put on my body whenever i was dancing. Some person would come up and say 'oh your Crumping!' then five years later 'oh your doing the Dougie!' then five years after that 'oh your Twerking!' - keep in mind when Im in a social setting i basically do the same dance movements ive been doing all my life in social dances! lol). So in a sense 'Free Jazz' was a statement or protest if you will of wanting to 'free' the form and expectation of what our cultural/racial/social backgrounds in dance designated us too. I was not wishing to erase any history but just augment it with the fact that my body in time is as much its own version of history adhering to shape, space, and time as it was any social construct being put onto it. I paired with the SF underground film boy queer genius Gary Fembot on this one. I was a queer punk as a teenager and had seen his films on underground film/zine mixtapes. I had also danced in a dance film of his that was an homage to 60's go-go boys called 'Mando Bottomless'. I told him what i wanted to do and he loved the idea and so together I directed and he filmed 'Free Jazz' in the space of a year. We wanted a dance mixtape that was the mid-way point between Mod, Punk, Surf, New Wave and Free Jazz dance interpretations". – Brontez Purnell

DRAWER DEPTH AND REAL ESTATE

PRAGEETA SHARMA

For Mark Stussy

Have you noticed that dresser drawers have gotten smaller?
It's in keeping with the real estate market, pay more for what you had
in some past life: the larger drawers of childhood.

Or perhaps you never had a deeper, wider, preponderant
clearing to open every morning.

Bedroom drawers and real estate engage in the same reduction.
Tempted by low interest rates for something you never
wanted until you made a comparison
thus initiating a consciousness in something
offhandedly morbid that won you over.

If you want to pay for bigger spaces — so you can fold with abandon or ecstasy
you have to shell out more money than you are comfortable with.
American real estate punctures your freedom with exiguous effort
and disastrous effects in order to re-organize your brain's desires.

I imagine the ratio is equal: 2 more inches is equivalent to 200 additional
square feet. Paying for the quality we might have misunderstood,
are we still children in this sense? Dresser drawers are no longer comforting,
expansive, and ordinary as the houses we now live in.

The box-drawn life we thought was so much bigger
than what is in front of us is outside and lives in our hungers.
I sigh and feel the world inching closer to my mortality button
and shove my clothes into the corners of all that will close a square.

UNFOLDING BEIJING

LAVINIA LIANG

I knew Beijing back when there was a pomegranate tree and something that counted as a front yard. In the kitchen annex, my grandmother and my aunt sliced cucumbers in half over the sink and taught me to eat them raw, juice running down our summer-parched chins. My grandmother told me about the rats that got in sometimes and how she killed them with her feet. I raised tadpoles with my first cousin in the tiny yard by placing them in cooking pots and feeding them rice, and we cried when it rained and we had to keep them outside. When they died, eventually, without ever growing legs, they died with little white pieces floating off from them — white matter that looked strangely like the rice we had fed them to keep them alive.

I knew Beijing in dreams and slivers — I was not born in Beijing and lived there only a short time. I was five or so the first time I visited; I remember a public toilet hole I almost fell into; a red bucket for bathing. In subsequent years, I would visit again, each visit spaced apart just enough for imagination to fill the gaps, like water. There was a hotel just down the alley, rounding a corner to comfort. When I found out over 10 years later that the hotel was real and not a constructed memory — although it had since closed for good — I was surprised.

"It is possible to long for a place you've never visited — to spend a lifetime nostalgic for a life you've never lived," Catherine Chung writes. For Chung, that place was the famed Wudang Mountains in central China, a place that filled her childhood fantasies. To apply the first part of Chung's idea — "a place you've never visited" — to how I feel about Beijing seems inaccurate. I have been to Beijing; in fact, I moved there for a year after I graduated from college and I loved saying that I *lived* there. But the nostalgia that Chung describes is still relevant to my relationship with Beijing — "nostalgic for a life you've never lived" — because I left the city.

Not long after I returned to the States, I opened a new library book. It was autumn, and the darkness outside belied the hour. "I walk through new commercial complexes constructed at Guomao, which look at once like big awkward gangsters gawking at one another [...] and I think, I belong here," I read in Xuan Juliana Wang's story "Days of Being Mild," collected in *Home Remedies*. What haunts me is the possibility of having stayed in the city, and of returning, and of ever possibly comprehending where a city is headed by only knowing what is has previously been.

Guomao! I know that place, too, I thought. Sitting backward on a northbound train, I nodded and smiled stupidly.

And then I knew what I was going to do.

I was going to collect all the English-language fiction on Beijing that I could.

¤

"I see an injustice: a Parisian does not have to bring his city out of nothingness every time he wants to describe it. A wealth of allusions lies at his disposal, for his city exists in works of word, birth, and chisel; even if it were to vanish from the face of the earth, one would still be able to recreate it in the imagination," Czesław Miłosz writes in his memoir, *Native Realm*. "But I, returning in thought to the streets where the most important part of my life unfolded, am obliged to invent the most utilitarian sort of symbols and am forced to condense my material."

This city of which Miłosz writes — the "city of his youth" — is Wilno, or Vilnius, the capital of Lithuania. This passage surfaced often in my mind as I began collecting, though I wondered if I really had Miłosz's same claim to obscurity. After all, I was concerned with Beijing, a city that Marco Polo had visited in the 13th century and described as "so vast, so rich and so beautiful, that no man on earth could design anything superior to it." It is also the current capital of the most populous country on earth. A city that, while hardly ever described in Polo's terms today, is nevertheless acknowledged as a place with which to be reckoned; a "behemoth," in the words of Chinese British novelist Xiaolu Guo. Jonathan Tel understood this same sense of scale and gravity when he

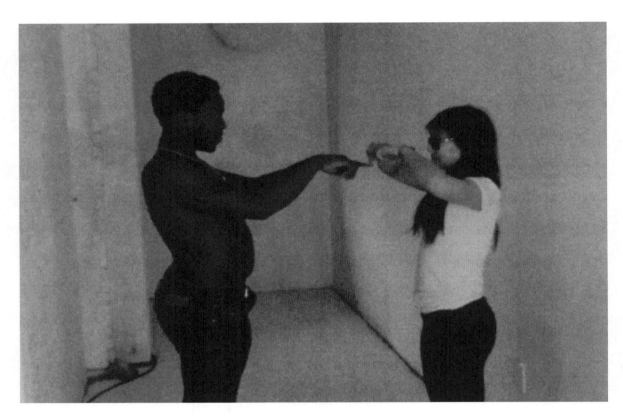

Brontez Purnell, still from *Free Jazz*, 2013, 8 mm film. Performed by Brontez Purnell Dance Company.

repurposed John Updike's famous quote for the fictionalized foreword of his own story collection *The Beijing of Possibilities*: "Beijing is the center of the universe […] 'The true Beijinger secretly believes that people living anywhere else have to be, in some sense, kidding.'"

With a history of several millennia, and home at present to over 21 million people, Beijing should be akin to Paris in at least some regards. Beijing is a city steeped in grandeur and exoticism, especially to foreign eyes. Given its political significance and its mythology, Beijing should be accessible in its symbolism; it should hold a treasury of referential works.

I say should. Because while I found a wealth of nonfiction books about Beijing available in English — biographies about the historic dynasties and their plumped-up palatial intrigue, photographic volumes of the hutongs where my grandparents lived, alternately dubious or surprisingly acute foreign policy analyses — I was confronted also by the comparative paucity of natively English or translated English literature about the city.

I did discover many novels and stories about places in China that were, well, not Beijing. This was heartening, because just as we do not truly need more books about or taking place in New York, we do not really *need* any more fiction about or taking place in Beijing. It is already the dominant setting for much, if not most, of Chinese-language literature and film. Rather, the world needs more stories about AIDS-afflicted villages in Henan, brutal winters in the Rust Belt of the Northeast, and e-waste dumping grounds in southern Guangdong. China, so often perceived as monolithic — and Beijing, often a metonymy for authoritarianism — needs variety, awareness, and humanity.

Yet, still, I continued searching for books that humanized this one particular city and revealed its specific nuances. I wanted stories that told me what I already knew and books that challenged me to leave myself behind. I desired what the filmmaker Edward Yang was once said to have done for 1960s Taiwan — to create a "completely immersive world." A world that would allow me to join personal memories to a larger collective of memories and, in so doing, make sense of them.

One story, early on, provided such an opportunity: Hao Jingfang's "Folding Beijing" — which was the first short story by a Chinese woman to win the Hugo Award, and which is collected in the English-language anthology *Invisible Planets*. In the story, Hao considers a Beijing divided into three "folds" so that the occupants of each fold never meet those who live in the others. At certain points during the day, the city flips so that one section hibernates underground. The story follows Lao Dao, a waste worker who crosses from his home in the Third Fold through the churning machinery of the city to the First Fold, where the lawns are pristine and cash comes in 10,000-yuan bills.

The story reminded me of my own time in Beijing. I, too, had navigated the folds of the city when I taught the children of migrant laborers, dined with local friends near our gym, and then attended gatherings that required a foreign passport — all in a week's time.

¤

Beijing itself has become a fiction. Let me get that out of the way. The city, like the nation for which it so often is a stand-in, is reducible to various fantasies. An economic fantasy — as a promise of financial betterment to migrants from all over the country; the culmination of the last 40 years of rapid development. A political fantasy — the appearance of total control. "Living in China is confusing now," the Chinese novelist Yan Lianke once aptly said. "It can feel like being in North Korea and the United States at the same time."

Fiction writer and former Beijing-based journalist Te-Ping Chen sharpens Yan's observation by identifying the effects of this reality on contemporary literature. "China is just a place that demands […] surrealism, hyper-realism, as well as realism," she says. "It's a place where the government literally will decide when it's going to rain […] which seems like a detail straight out of a science fiction novel, but it's real life in Beijing."

Chen's own fiction engages head-on with these multiple "genres" of reality. Take, for example, her story "New Fruit," from the collection *Land of Big Numbers*, the local setting of which is unnamed, and yet which evokes so easily the publicly intimate life of Beijing's hutongs, or alleyways. One woman, for instance, is known for gossiping while she squats on the communal latrines. The whole story is told in the collective first person: *we*. The entire community observes and participates, much as things truly are in hutong neighborhoods. One day, in a surrealist turn of events, a hybridized fruit appears on the streets, and eating it causes its consumers to experience particular emotions. The first crop of fruit helps its consumers develop sunnier dispositions; romances even rekindle. But a later crop causes darker feelings, like remorse, to surface. The power of "New Fruit" lies not only in how convincingly it portrays a nonexistent fruit, but also in how it toes the line between traditional "realism" and the hyper-realism that Chen attributes to China. If the weather can be custom-tailored to the extent that it is in Beijing, why can't fruit?

A similarly absurd but firmly realist foil to "New Fruit" is the story "Lulu" from the same collection. "Lulu" follows fraternal twins who take separate paths — one becomes a professional video game player and the other a political activist. Lulu, the political activist, is living in Beijing when she is detained, interrogated, and beaten. Upon her release, she resumes her online activities, and is subsequently arrested. There is no wiggle room in "Lulu"; no possibility of hiding behind a symbolic object, as there is in "New Fruit" — the threats to Lulu's life and the injuries she sustains from her interrogation are real. Her twin brother asks her to stop what she is doing, even as he understands that their reality, one which does not tolerate dissent, is untenable. He knows, too, that both of their lives — his, withdrawn into virtual worlds, and hers, hyperreal and high risk — are two extreme responses to that reality.

Beijing's visibility as a city means that it often functions as a totem for this everyday social dissonance that can be found throughout the country. In Xiaolu Guo's *Twenty Fragments of a Ravenous Youth*, the young narrator Fenfang, who calls herself a "peasant," moves to Beijing in a classic attempt to reinvent herself. She counts herself among the millions of China's so-called "floating population" of rural migrants who have moved to urban areas in search of opportunity. During her first day there, Fenfang hears a mother and daughter arguing in a nearby house. Suddenly, the door flies open and both women rush out, only to be immediately hit and crushed by a van in the street. To Fenfang's shock, the driver of the van pulls the mother and daughter into the back of his vehicle and, "without saying anything or looking at me, he drove off."

Guo's novel is a modern view on the impersonal side of the city, its injustices, and its breakneck speed of both change and daily life. Lao She — the pen name of Shu Qingchun and one of the preeminent Chinese literary figures of the 20th century — provides a look at 1920s Beijing through his novel *Rickshaw Boy*. Many of the scenes in *Rickshaw Boy* are miserable. The protagonist is the poor, orphaned rickshaw driver Xiangzi, who encounters misfortune again and again until he simply gives up trying to be ethical or good. Beijing is also a character, and is described simultaneously as "filthy" and "beautiful," "chaotic" and "idle." *Twenty Fragments of a Ravenous Youth* and *Rickshaw Boy*, although written in vastly different contexts and very different Beijings, contain similar ideas: Beijing is unforgiving. It is often inhumane, and it often makes no sense.

There are volumes of English-language "Shanghai literature" on my shelf, too — like André Malraux's *Man's Fate* and Jenny Zhang's *Sour Heart*. But Shanghai is Shanghai; it is clear in the Western imagination. It has not wavered in the same way that Beijing has, so constantly out of focus. Shanghai has the Bund, for goodness's sake, and its past is not muddied with the unspeakable nor its present reduced to being a synonym for totalitarianism in a foreign news headline. "Foreigners have always come to Shanghai in order to feel that they are living on the verge of the future," critic Moira Weigel claims. In contrast, I think people come to Beijing seeking the past — to make sense of it.

¤

As my collection grew, I found that a sizable proportion of available Anglophone literature on Beijing focuses on one particular matter: the 1989 Tiananmen Square pro-democracy protests. Ma Jian's *Beijing Coma* tells the story of a young protestor who falls into a coma and prepares to awake 10 years later, Rip Van Winkle-style, to an unrecognizable China. Baoshu's novella "What Has Passed Shall in Kinder Light Appear," collected in the science fiction anthology *Broken Stars*, features a narrator who participates in the protests with his beloved. Ha Jin's *The Crazed* closes with the protagonist's attendance at the demonstrations, while Hong Ying's *Summer of Betrayal* begins with the protagonist fleeing the aftermath. Yiyun Li's *Kinder Than Solitude* features a character who is involved in the 1989 protests and who, shortly after, is poisoned, almost to death. Meng Jin's *Little Gods* opens on a bird's-eye view of the capital on the eve of last day of the protests, preparing us for what we, but not the characters, know is imminent: "From above, the heart of the city is easy to see. Beijing is a bull's-eye."

Madeleine Thien's *Do Not Say We Have Nothing* recounts in detail those fateful months: the before, the during, the after. Thien describes the elasticity of the days and nights leading up to June 1989, when the whole city seemed to "come together," in a book that spans generations and continents and grasps at a national history. The tale is told through the lives of three talented musicians — the most talented among them a young composer named Sparrow. Thien's ambitious novel is set in a number of locations, including Vancouver, Shanghai, a village outside Changsha, another village called Bingpai, a village in Guangxi, and the beautiful and perilous western deserts of Gansu.

But the story's most demanding moments are set in Beijing. Beijing's importance is first foreshadowed in the name of the street on which Sparrow and his family lived when he was a young student in Shanghai — Beijing Road. The story homes in on Beijing like a compass pointing north. Upon returning to Beijing Road in Shanghai after the Cultural Revolution, Sparrow's mother finds her entire family missing. In her despair, she smashes all the crockery in the house: "She did it carefully, disposing of her favorites immediately, all the while singing: 'Comrades, amputate the branches and tear down the leaves…' Her neighbors thought she had lost her mind…"

Years later, in Beijing itself, Sparrow's daughter Ai-ming finds herself swept up in the fervor and yearning of the pro-democracy movements. In the midst of the Tiananmen protests, Sparrow thinks to himself: "What had any of them done that was criminal? Hadn't they done their best to listen and to believe? There was nothing in his hands and never have been."

A collapse of time and distance is briefly triggered in the mirrored absurdity experienced by mother and son. The text asks readers to consider: Have things always been this way? And will things ever be different?

¤

Some parts of daily life and society *are* changing; that much is true. Buildings and structures everywhere in China are being torn down to make way for new developments. Residential, commercial, and even touristic "heritage" sites are all being dissembled or remade or both. The journalist Peter Hessler, writing for *The New Yorker* in 2007, wrote about how "chai," or demolition, has become its own sort of "culture" in China over the years. The Chinese character for chai, 拆, has become the literal writing on the wall: it appears on structures overnight as if written by invisible hands; sometimes the character is spray-painted, sometimes it is chalked. There had been talks for years about "chai"-ing the houses in my grandparents' neighborhood when, suddenly, at the end of my time in Beijing, they came for my grandparents' house.

One of Hessler's neighbors in Beijing used to say, "We live in *Chai nar*." The phrase sounds like "China" to the Anglophone ear, but in Chinese it means, "Demolish where?" As Hessler writes: "It was only a matter of time before the government *chai*'d more buildings in our area, but [my neighbor] never dwelled on the future. More than four decades in *Chai nar* had taught him that nothing lasts forever."

Nothing lasts, but collecting, perhaps, is a way to counteract that: to stop time, to hold, to embody; to encompass the wholeness of something — of a city, and its corresponding imaginary. And to retain the truth of history. If authorities attempt to rewrite the past, then the burden of keeping alive the stories of individuals — and the truth — falls, at least partially, to writers. Throughout the course of my collecting, I have wondered how much I lose in pursuing works about a Chinese city that are either written natively in English or are translated into English. But if Chinese is not currently a viable language for truth, then perhaps other languages can be cradles for the time being. And I see now that I am also learning and knowing Beijing

Brontez Purnell, still from *Free Jazz*, 2013, 8 mm film. Performed by Brontez Purnell Dance Company.

from the outside in. Folding and unfolding. Two actions that — as Hao Jingfang may very well also know — when seen from different perspectives, might just be interchangeable.

In those final days of my grandparents' house, I wandered through the gutted residences and took pictures of everything. A single Croc shoe that had been left behind. Suitcases filled with papers that were already half-dust. A plastic pitcher, still upright. I asked the demolition workers if I could take a picture of them on break. I was terrified of forgetting anything. Simultaneously, I was fearful that, like Dai Wei from *Beijing Coma*, I would remember everything but have nothing to show for it; that I would forever "wander back and forth through the space between [my] flesh and [my] memories."

As Susan Orlean observes in *The Library Book*: "In the library, time is dammed up — not just stopped but saved." Orlean may be considering the library as a location as much as the library as an idea, but of course, what is a library if not a collection?

¤

I think now that one, or perhaps *the*, reason English-language literature on Beijing was difficult to find is because Beijing is difficult to write about. Because it is difficult to love. I can't think of a single foreigner who has told me that they loved Beijing; perhaps they found the city striking or imposing or interesting, but not lovable. Folks will first tentatively ask, "And did you like your time in Beijing?" before they explain to me why they didn't enjoy theirs. Young Chinese people tell me that they'll do their time in Beijing and then they'll leave. Go south to Chengdu

or something, where the weather and social conditions are fairer.

"There was something terribly unromantic about falling in love in Beijing," Peter Tieryas Liu writes in a story titled, simply, "A Beijing Romance" and collected in *Watering Heaven*. The city, with its harsh superblock architecture, and the Forbidden City and Tiananmen Square as its hollow hearts, poses in direct contrast to the soft, traditional romance of — and here, the same unwarranted comparison — Paris. As a character in *Little Gods* observes, wrestling with her own biases and fear of those biases: "The scale of infrastructure here surpassed the ability of my body. Beijing was not built for humans, I thought — and here my mind completed the idea, even as I heard my other self saying, *What a derivative, Western thought* — but for military machines."

Beijing is unromantic, and difficult to love, and hardly livable, and absurd. "And yet Beijing was the most romantic city I'd known," continues Liu's narrator in "A Beijing Romance." Why? Because: "Several million people were squeezed into the metropolis that was undergoing constant surgery on its ruptured streets [but] somehow, beneath the grandeur of it all, there was love: strident, audacious love."

Beijing's beauty comes from its hallmark of perseverance — of persisting and finding the heart to continue giving to others amid the city's sheer magnitude and harsh living conditions. Collecting the literature of Beijing helps us to keep the past alive, and to capture and hold close the real, human lives that have passed through the city. It provides an entry point for us to begin to make sense of that history, both social and personal; as the protagonist of Xu Zechen's *Running Through Beijing* says, upon being released from prison: "Anywhere was fine as long as it was in Beijing."

Most importantly, however, creating this body of literature is a way forward. Nothing lasts. But these stories show where we've been. They leave a trail for others to follow — and show them where to begin.

Brontez Purnell, still from *Free Jazz*, 2013, 8 mm film. Performed by Brontez Purnell Dance Company.

CHORUS

NATASHA RAO

A cul-de-sac of televisions
switched to the same channel.
Overhead, the bleating of geese.
Attention, these days, is held
for a brief moment, the way
I might hold onions
at the market. I watch the stock
simmer on the stove. I gather,
refresh, then trade
the screen for the window,
where snow is falling decisively
in the same direction. Look
away, look back, it's already done.
I fling wide the door to feel
which way the wind is moving,
barely open my mouth before
a new species of bird evolves
and fills the air
with uncountable versions
of the freshest song.

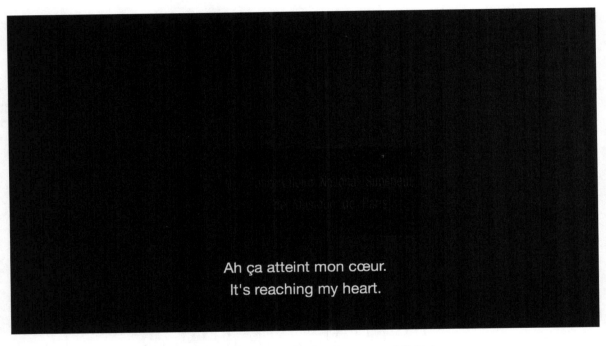

Mona Varichon, *La Cité des arts, Épisode 4, Les couloirs/The corridors*, 2021, HD video, color, stereo sound, 07:42 min. This is the fourth episode in a four episode mini-series commissioned by MycoTV for the ICA London's Cinema 3 broadcast. Set at the Cité Internationale des Arts, the series examines its potential as a meeting ground, informal teaching and learning environment, and a political space. In this episode, we follow Cité resident Nicolas Faubert through corridors filled with the sounds of rehearsing musicians while he relates a recent encounter with the police.

LANGUAGE LESSONS

NANCY KRICORIAN

Our house in Watertown was built on a double lot, with the front door on Walnut Street and the back door on Lincoln. We lived oriented toward Lincoln Street, where in our large backyard, my father tended a vegetable garden, and my grandmother managed the annual beds and the perennials — lilacs, forsythia, viburnum, two types of hydrangeas, and three kinds of roses. There were two pear trees, a peach tree, and a grape vine that climbed up the house and grew over one side of the second-story porch.

This porch was where my grandmother stored her large pickle crock under an enamel-topped table. In spring, summer, and autumn, she sat on a vinyl-covered couch watching over the yard and the neighbors. In addition to the wood-framed clothesline in the back yard, my grandmother also strung a rope above her porch railing where she hung dish-towels and clothes out to dry. She stored the wooden clothespins in a bag she had fashioned from a dress that I had worn as a toddler. She had sewn closed the hem of the dress and suspended it from the line on a wire hanger.

Many of the families on Lincoln Street were Armenian — Masoyan, Moushigian, Kazanjian, Kasparian, Kricorian, Mekjian, and Gayzagian — and the ones who weren't my grandmother referred to not by name, but by nationality: the Greek, the Irish, the Italian, and the Portuguese. Many of the surrounding houses were built as single-family dwellings, but ours was a three-story, two-family house. My father and his three siblings had grown up in the top two floors. When I was grow-ing up, my grandmother and my father's youngest brother lived there. My parents, my sister, and I inhabited the ground floor.

We were officially two separate households, with two independent apart-ments, and in the basement, there were even two washing machines, one for my grandmother and one for my mother. But we were one family. My sister and I were often upstairs with my grandmother — watching old Shirley Temple movies in her living room or sitting on her back porch eating watermelon or pelting but-ternuts at a brazen squirrel that was feast-ing in the pear tree. There was another second-story porch on the front of the house, and sometimes I took a nap or read a book on a day bed there because it was quiet and shaded by an enormous spruce tree that grew in the front yard.

My grandmother would pound with a broom handle on the floor of her apartment by the utility closet, calling for my father, "Eddie!" He would open the closet in our apartment and shout, "What is it, Ma?" She replied, "I'm sending the bucket." Either my sister or I would be dispatched to our back porch as a plastic bucket tied to a length of clothesline rope descended. Inside we might find a pot of fresh-made yogurt, a basket of fresh *cheo-reg* sweet rolls, or a plastic bag filled with *manta*, tiny meat dumplings shaped like boats.

Our family attended the United Armenian Brethren Church on Arlington Street in Watertown. It had been found-ed and built in 1938 by Armenians from Cilicia, most of them Genocide survi-vors, and was led the Reverend Vartan Bilezikian until his retirement in the early 1950s. My grandfather Levon (Leo) Kricorian, who had been one of the founders of Watertown's St. James Armenian Apostolic Church in the ear-ly '30s, had converted to Protestantism and was also among the founders of the Brethren Church.

During my grandfather's days, our family pew was the second one from the front on the right-hand side, but after his death and with the arrival of my squirmy sister, we moved to the left-hand side, second from the back. In this second lo-cation, the Amiralians sat behind us, the Haroutunians were in front of us, and the Bilezekians were across the aisle.

By the time I was seven, the church had been renamed the Watertown Evangelical Church and Reverend Proctor Davis, a Southern Baptist who resembled evange-list Billy Graham, held sway from the pul-pit. When we sang from the hymnal, the Armenian widows in the front row with their black hats and white buns chorused in a minor key.

¤

In elementary school, many of my close friends were Armenian. I watched with envy on Monday and Wednesday afternoons at the end of the school day as they marched off together for Armenian language lessons at the cultural center attached to the St. James Church. My grandmother had offered to pay my Armenian school tuition, but my mother, who was French Canadian, made clear without words that she preferred I decline the offer. This was another silent skirmish by proxy in the power struggle between my mother and my grandmother.

My mother never learned Armenian, despite living in the same house with her Armenian mother-in-law. My grandmother and father often spoke the language together, or rather my grandmother spoke to him in Armenian and he replied in English. The fact that my mother knew hardly one word of Armenian when the language flowed around her in our house, in the neighborhood, and at church was remarkable. Recently, I asked her why she had never learned it, and she said, "They didn't accept me because I wasn't Armenian, and I didn't want to know what they were saying about me."

My father's first language was Armenian, but when he went to kindergarten, he spoke more Turkish than English because his paternal grandmother who spoke only Turkish lived with his family. My mother's first language was French, but she was shamed out of speaking it when she went to elementary school, and she lost almost all of it after she was sent to an orphanage at age eight.

I knew a little Armenian — or rather I knew several dozen phrases in Armenian and some random words. My grandmother taught me how to count to 10 in Armenian, but beyond that I learned through hearing certain phrases over and again. I understood my grandmother's commands — give me a spoon of sugar, shut the door, open the light, take this, come here, sit there, stay there, walk, run, hurry up, go slowly — without knowing the language. I understood what she was saying when she called my uncle a squash head. It was clear that the word *amot* meant shame and when she said *amot kezi* I knew that I was or had done something shameful. This generally involved my *vardik* (underwear) or my *vorik* (bottom), and often specifically referred to my ballet and tapdancing outfits. She also said, often, in English, "Cover your shame."

Her English was heavily accented and full of grammatical errors and mispronunciations, and I cringed at the thought that anyone outside our family would hear her mistakes, particularly her misuse of the personal pronouns he and she. One time she said to me, "Your mother, he is not a lazy woman." It never occurred to me that I should wonder why these gendered pronouns gave her so much trouble. She also called window wipers *vipers*, and instead of throw she said *trow*, as in *trow dees een dee ash barrel*.

I loved my Armenian grandmother, but I wanted to be as American as possible and to speak perfect English. When I was about 10 years old I started wishing that I were a White Anglo-Saxon Protestant with a simple, muscular last name that didn't broadcast my family's immigrant origins. This was probably as much at the heart of my not going to Armenian school as my mother's disapproval. I kept my distance from the recently arrived Armenian kids from Beirut with their accents and their mismatched clothes. Some of the other kids — particularly the Irish and Italians, whose whiteness was relatively recently established — picked on the Armenians, calling them insulting names such as F.O.B., which I thought was an acronym involving a swear word, but eventually learned meant fresh off the boat. One day in the parking lot after school I saw a tough girl named Dana surrounded by a scrum of kids as she slapped around a dowdily dressed immigrant girl with the unfortunate name of Pearlene.

In fifth grade, our teacher asked us each to bring in a homemade food that represented our ethnic backgrounds. My grandmother, who was an excellent cook, baked a batch of *gurabia*, Armenian butter cookies dusted with confectioner's sugar. She carefully packed them in a tin lined with waxed paper. As I walked to school carrying the cookie tin, I felt a growing sense of dread. I was sure my Armenian classmates would find the cookies to be ordinary and the non-Armenian kids would think they were bland and disgusting, so unlike the Oreos and Chips Ahoy! that they brought in their lunchboxes. I left the *gurabia* in my locker. I knew that I couldn't bring them home with me. A few days later, I dumped them in a trashcan.

I remember being shocked when an Irish boy named Howie, who lived in the projects, called me an "Armo camel driver" and an "Armo rugbeater." Howie had somehow seen beyond my impeccable English and the clothes I had carefully chosen at the Jordan Marsh department store. He had magically surmised that my grandmother spoke fractured English and that my father came home from his meat cutter job with dried blood on his cuffs and bits of hamburger and sawdust in the seams of his shoes.

In junior high school, I signed up for French class. My grandmother told me that after the Deportations she had learned French in the orphanage. "*Comment allez-vous?*" she said to me. This was also my mother's first language, although the only vestiges of it that I witnessed was on our monthly visits to the tarpaper shack in New Hampshire where her bedridden father growled in a language I couldn't understand and my maternal cousins referred to my mother as "*Ma tount.*"

But my mother's French and the French at school were two very different things. At the time, French was the language that all the serious students studied, and it was considered very classy. Classier still was our French class's field trip to Du Barry Restaurant on Newberry Street in Boston, where incidentally I was horrified to discover that people ate snails, frog legs, and rabbits.

At Watertown High School, Mrs. Yacoubian offered Armenian classes, but no one I knew in the college track signed up for them. I developed a rapport with my French teacher, Monsieur Craig, who wore a beard and a beret, and made allusions to some mysterious suffering he had endured during World War II. He loaned me books by Jean-Paul Sartre, and I sometimes stayed after class to discuss French existentialism with him. He said to me, "You and I are intellectuals," dismissing the football cheerleaders as anti-intellectual riffraff.

¤

I wanted to escape Watertown High School and those cheerleaders who carried red and white pompons to homeroom on the days we were forced to the auditorium for football pep rallies. I was

Mona Varichon, *La Cité des art, Épisode 2, Les cours/Classes*, 2021, HD video, color, stereo sound, 09:54 min. This is the second episode in a four episodes mini-series commissioned by MycoTV for the ICA London's Cinema 3 broadcast. Set at the Cité Internationale des Arts, the series examines its potential as a meeting ground, informal teaching and learning environment, and a political space. In this episode, we follow residents and non-residents as they attend freestyle dance workshops led by Cité resident Nicolas Faubert.

tired of the old Armenian ladies at church who looked out of the sides of their eyes at the scandalous length of my skirt. I hoped to find other people who had read *The Brothers Karamazov*.

When I left for college three hours from home, I kitted myself out in wide-wale corduroys, button down shirts, and Fair Isle sweaters, naïvely believing this was an effective disguise. Maybe it was growing up, maybe it was my wealthy American boyfriend telling me I wasn't fooling anyone, or maybe it was living for a term with a *pied noir* family in Toulouse during a foreign study program, but by my second year in college I felt more Armenian than ever.

I interviewed my grandmother for an oral history project that was assigned in a class on Mothers and Daughters in literature. Sitting on the second-story back porch, shaded by the grapevine, she told me the story of what had happened to her family when they were driven from Mersin during the Deportations and Massacres. It was the first time she had told anyone in the family the details of her parents' deaths and how she had managed to survive. The history of this familial and communal trauma had suffused the air that I breathed growing up in Watertown's Armenian community, while never having been articulated. Now my grandmother's voice was in my head telling the story. It was both a burden and a legacy.

My grandmother died at the end of my first year at a graduate writing program in New York City. That summer I went to talk with her oldest friend, Alice Kharibian, who had been with my grandmother at the concentration camp in the Syrian desert outside Ras al-Ain when they were girls. Alice said, "Your grandmother was so wishy-washy. I was *jarbig*

(clever, resourceful) for all of us. She and her brother would have been dead in the desert without me." Now I had Alice's voice sounding in my head along with my grandmother's.

¤

Back at the university the following autumn I enrolled in my first Armenian language class. I realized then that my grandmother's confusion about he and she was due to the fact that in Armenian the third person singular pronoun is gender neutral. I was again surrounded by Armenians and the Armenian language, this time by choice. I began writing about my grandmother, and I wrote poems in her voice and in the voices of other women from our church. I remember reading out loud in Sharon Olds's workshop a prose poem I drafted a few months after my grandmother died. Entitled "The Angel," it started, "My grandmother is in heaven. This heaven has no Turks, no women in skimpy bathing suits, no squirrels in the pear trees."

Later, I switched genres to fiction and began drafting the interlocking stories that would become my first novel, *Zabelle*, which was a fictionalized account of my grandmother's life as a Genocide survivor and immigrant bride. When the novel was published, many Armenians came to my book tour events around the country. Zabelle Chahasbanian was a stand-in for many people's beloved mother or grandmother, so the book was popular in the community.

During the question-and-answer sessions after these readings, I was repeatedly asked about my credentials: "Are you *all* Armenian? Do you speak Armenian? Is your husband Armenian? Do you know how to make *cheoreg*?" It was the first time that I was made to feel that I wasn't Armenian enough. At one event, a man in the audience stood up to denounce me, saying, "You're not Armenian. You're an American writer exploiting your grandmother's story to make money." I replied, "If you calculated the number of hours that I spent writing this book and divided it into the advance I received, I made less than minimum wage. If I wanted to make money, I'd write porn." The absurdity of what he said was apparent, but it stung because I was ashamed about having failed my grandmother. I was not a good Armenian girl, I hadn't produced Armenian children, and I was in fact some kind of mongrel. If I spoke fluent Armenian, I might have been forgiven the rest.

Over the years, I continued studying the Armenian language at the Armenian Diocese, at the Prelacy, and then with three excellent private tutors, one after the other. I learned the alphabet, I was able to read at a first-grade level, and I could write simple paragraphs in the present tense. But I still couldn't carry on a more than basic conversation. I should have studied harder. I should have gone to one of those language immersion programs in Venice or Jerusalem or Beirut. But I was living my American life, raising my American children, writing my Armenian-themed American novels, and working first as an adjunct writing instructor, then as a literary scout for European publishers, and later as an organizer for a women's peace group.

Here I am decades later still studying Armenian. It's a language rooted in my childhood, forever echoing with the sound of my grandmother's voice. I have loved discovering the ways that the expressions and words I learned from her are part of the vast and intricate network of Western Armenian, a language that has the sturdiness and delicacy of a needle lace tablecloth, but one that is categorized by UNESCO as "definitely endangered."

For the past four years, I've been taking private lessons over Skype with Sosy, a teacher who fled Aleppo for Yerevan because of the Syrian Civil War. I have finally learned the simple past and the imperfect tenses. I have been writing micro-stories in Armenian, which Sosy proofreads and corrects. Recently she said to me, "Now you have the grammar, you understand the workings of the language, you just need more vocabulary. You need to listen, and to talk, talk, talk."

I keep walking this long road back to my grandmother. Talking to myself as I walk, I eventually end up climbing the steps to the back porch of her house in heaven, where together she and I will roll stuffed grape leaves at the enamel-topped table as we talk and talk in her native tongue.

THE MANY SOULS OF CLARICE LISPECTOR'S TRANSLATORS

SARAH MCEACHERN

Clarice Lispector remains distinctive as a writer for numerous reasons: her crackling language, the complex ideas bounding off the page, her disregard for classification, the vulnerable intimacy of her narrators' interior thoughts. Another place where she sets herself apart is the epigraph addressed to her readers in her 1964 novel, *The Passion According to G.H.* In the 2012 translation by Idra Novey, part of this epigraph reads, "I would be happy if this book were only read by people whose souls are already formed. Those who know that the approach, of whatever it may be, happens gradually and painstakingly — even passing through the opposite of what it approaches." Uninterested in catering to or coddling the reader, or for her writing to be simply consumed for entertainment, Clarice demands the reader at attention, pushing her reader to consider their soul before they even pick up her book. How many spoiled readers have mistaken this note for a clever ploy? Only to find themselves consumed by Clarice, given fair warning and still unprepared.

When I had the chance to speak with Idra, she told me *The Passion According to G.H.* was her first Clarice novel, having read it years before learning Portuguese and taking on the project of its translation. The narrator, only identified as G.H., undergoes a spiritual and mystical journey upon finding a cockroach in her maid's bedroom, offering a kaleidoscopic exploration reaching deep into her own humanity. Idra read the novel for a college class on experimental Latin American writing by women, and said, "Finding Clarice Lispector unlocked a door for me. I went to Brazil to learn Portuguese to read her work in the original. Her work just really spoke to me. She was really pivotal in what I wanted to do as a writer." Idra's eventual translation of *The Passion According to G.H.* was one of the first reissued in New Directions Publishing's project of retranslating Clarice's novels, as well as some of her novels which were translated into English for the first time.

Katrina Dodson, the translator of Clarice's *Complete Stories*, also cites *The Passion According to G.H.* as her first Clarice novel. After moving to Brazil and beginning to learn Portuguese, Katrina read the novel on a trip down the Amazon River while sleeping in a hammock on the boat. She thinks of *The Passion According to G.H.* as Clarice's most challenging novel, both emotionally and intellectually. Clarice herself considered it the most

suited to her as a writer among her nine novels. Early in the novel, the narrator tells us, "If I confirm myself and consider myself truthful, I'll be lost because I won't know where to inlay my new way of being." This idea of being lost builds throughout the book, another way of framing the spiritual transformation or the cockroach-induced metamorphosis G.H. goes through, which often provokes an association between Clarice's writing and Franz Kafka's. Later, G.H. confides, "I am so afraid that I can only accept that I got lost if I imagine that someone is holding my hand." If my hand were held along G.H.'s journey by anyone, it was likely Idra Novey, whose translation brought Clarice's novel to my attention.

Doubting my own soul while reading *The Passion According to G.H.*, I found myself caught up thinking about Idra's soul. What had been the state of her soul when she first encountered Clarice's writing in college, when she set out to learn Portuguese to read it in its original, or when she started translating the novel years later? Perhaps what I most longed to know about Idra's soul was what it looked like *after* she had translated the novel. What had the process of translation done to the souls of Clarice Lispector's translators; how did they themselves transform in order to bring Clarice's novels into a language that I could read — then transforming me?

When I spoke to Johnny Lorenz, the translator of Clarice's posthumous novel, *A Breath of Life*, he returned to the same epigraph. "I'll confess that the first time I read *The Passion According to G.H.*, I was not ready for it. Perhaps my soul was not yet fully formed. Sometimes, you must come back to a book — when you are no longer the same reader, the same person." Johnny later told me he first stumbled onto Clarice in a used bookstore as a graduate student, finding a book of Clarice's short writing for the *Jornal do Brasil*, written during the '60s and '70s. Years later, having now become her translator, Johnny said, "I don't think my soul is fully formed (whatever that might mean), but I know that now, when the narrator of that book asks to hold my hand before her terrible journey begins, I'm ready to give it to her." Trusting Clarice, who begins already suspicious of your soul, is a similar theme among her translators, although their interactions with Clarice's works, their translating processes, and their backgrounds are vast and varied experiences.

Magdalena Edwards, a co-translator of *The Chandelier*, said, "Lispector is an incredibly generous writer, to her readers and her translators." I have read several of the translated novels from New Directions, and Clarice's translators are always far from my mind. Each of their distinctions blend together to create a similar voice of Clarice through her novels. Alison Entrekin, the translator of Clarice's first novel, *Near to the Wild Heart*, mentioned that in Clarice's previous translations, "She was tidied up a lot in the past. In her original translations, to my ear, she sounds like an older English writer, and not the Clarice I knew from the Portuguese."

Elizabeth Bishop was one of Clarice's earliest translators, publishing three of her short stories in *The Kenyon Review* in the 1960s, but Clarice's novels were translated throughout the '80s and the '90s, published by academic presses in the United States as well as New Directions. Her most recent group of interlocutors reflected translators with more diverse backgrounds than simply academic, as well as emulated by a more global world. Johnny Lorenz, Magdalena Edwards, and Katrina Dodson grew up with immigrant parents, which offered exposure to different languages spoken around the home. Idra Novey, Johnny, and Katrina grew up throughout distinctive American regions (Appalachia, Florida, and California, respectively), while Magdalena grew up in Chicago, Los Angeles, and Washington, DC. She speaks English with a West Coast– and Los Angeles–inflected accent. Alison Entrekin grew up in Australia, where she lives now. Language — as one must admit when they're working with Clarice, and as Katrina later echoed to me during our conversation — is boundless. Clarice herself grew up with parents who learned Portuguese around the same time she did after they immigrated from what's now modern Ukraine during her infancy. Her parents used Yiddish at home, although Clarice herself didn't speak it. Portuguese was her native language, but she spoke it with a lisp, which she passed off as a mysterious, foreign accent, only adding to her own mythos.

Her translators' relationships to Portuguese are similarly diverse and non-singular. Alison Entrekin moved to Brazil after studying creative writing as an undergraduate, with the aim to become an academic, although her focus quickly shifted to translation, which she studied in São Paulo. She said, "Translation is an incredible school of Portuguese, and I was also getting full immersion in the language living in Brazil, being married to a Brazilian, and surrounded by the Brazilian people and culture." Her sojourn in Brazil was originally intended to be two years but ended up lasting 24. Likewise, Katrina

Mona Varichon, *23 mars 2019 Gilets Jaunes Acte XIX*, 2020, HD video, color, stereo sound, 11:23 min. Composed entirely of Instagram stories gathered on March 23rd, 2019, this video follows Yellow Vests, tourists and Parisians going about their Saturdays, at times determined, irritated, fearful and enchanted.

Dodson moved to Brazil in 2003, leaving behind America during the early Bush years. She noted, "Both Vietnamese and Portuguese are more personal languages to me, since I first came to them in the course of daily life and only later studied them in a classroom."

Katrina's relationship with Portuguese feels like its own kaleidoscopic metamorphosis. She said, "I feel a lot of emotional resonance with Portuguese. Even though it's not my family language, it's a language I inhabited in my early 20s during a big adventure living in Rio de Janeiro." After teaching English in Brazil, Katrina began to take classes at Rio's Pontifical Catholic University, studying Portuguese more seriously by reading Brazilian literature. In 2004, she returned to the United States, in part to pursue a PhD in Comparative Literature at UC Berkeley, and her later trips to Brazil became focused on research, including living there again in 2011 through 2012 on a Fulbright-Hays dissertation fellowship. "There was a major shift in my relationship to Portuguese, from being more personal when I was reading for pleasure and speaking it just to get around Rio, to later when I was training to be a scholar, reading Brazilian literature to master the field while constructing arguments and interpretations."

While Katrina identifies Portuguese as a personal language since she didn't begin learning it in a classroom, Johnny, the child of Brazilian immigrants, used the same words to describe his own relationship to the language. He said, "My formal education happened in English-speaking classrooms; I would learn Portuguese during family cook-outs and parties, or on trips to Brazil to visit family, or listening to Brazilian CDs on my local visits to Tower Records." He would later go on to earn a PhD in English Literature from The University of Texas at Austin, in addition to pursuing a Fulbright to conduct research in Brazil. Magdalena additionally cemented her relationship with Portuguese by way of a PhD program, although she mentions having an emotional connection to the language that started during childhood. Born in Santiago and raised by Chilean parents in the United States, she was regularly exposed to Portuguese, often through music. She said, "As I got older and started to connect the dots of childhood, I realized that my parents had spent their honeymoon in Rio de Janeiro in 1976, the year before Clarice Lispector died. Surely this could not be a total coincidence." When she first went to Rio to conduct research on Elizabeth Bishop and Clarice, she said, "It felt like a homecoming." Like Magdalena, Idra was likewise drawn to Brazil and Portuguese in large part with the desire to better understand Clarice.

Clarice offers many ideas about writing and language to her translators, which many of them have carried into their own creative works. Idra's novel, *Ways to Disappear* (Little, Brown and Company, 2016), is about a translator in search of the writer she's working on, who has disappeared into an almond tree in a park in Rio. Her book of poems, *Clarice: The Visitor* (Sylph Editions, 2014), is written as letters directly to Clarice, interrogating translation and visitations. Idra said, "Clarice is always working toward the ineffable. As a writer, I always follow where she went as a writer — something that I feel ambivalent about, something I cannot find resolution about. That's where Clarice goes." While translating *The Passion According to G.H.*, Idra began drafting her first novel. Regarding the relationship between her work as a translator and her work as a writer, Idra said, "I think translation is one of the deepest kinds of reading. You have to really inhabit the mind of the writer as much as you can, and as a result, I think it's an apprenticeship."

Magdalena's performance work and her own writing often revolve around what it means to be a creative and a translator, as well as where these two practices interfold. With regards to Clarice, Magdalena said, "She has marked my creative practice indelibly — as a writer, translator, performer, mother, and sentient creature." Magdalena has incorporated her experiences translating Clarice into performance pieces. In her one-woman show *I Wanna Be Robert De Niro*, Clarice and the protagonist of Clarice's novel *The Chandelier*, Virginia, return to Magdalena in her daydreams, demanding she return to their translations. The piece was performed at the Hollywood Fringe Festival, and she performed a second piece, *The Body Speaks: On Clarice Lispector's The Chandelier*, at Oxford University.

When I asked Katrina if she felt like translating Clarice had an impact on her life, she told me, "Completely." She sees her project translating Clarice's short stories as a defining moment in her life. Katrina said, "She's emotionally demanding, and I felt very wrapped up in her world. For two years, the most important person in my life was this dead writer. I learned so much about writing, about all the things you can do in a sentence."

Johnny has consistently returned to Clarice's approach to writing in the opening pages of *A Breath of Life*, saying, "Those pages had quite an effect on me as a reader and as a writer. In these opening pages, the book itself is telling us that it does not want to be 'liked.' I've thought about this

a lot — to write beyond the desire to be liked." His answer came full circle, and I found myself back at the ideas in *The Passion According to G.H.*'s epigraph. How its simple few lines pivot the entire expectation of how readers approach books — as serviceable objects. The formation and maturity of a reader is held just as responsible as the writer's craft. Clarice's novels find a great diversity among each other, ruminating on an ever-changing interpretation of what it means to be a reader, a writer, a novelist. These roles constantly reinvent from novel to novel. Translation itself offers an expansion on literature, especially when novels move away from the confines of the Western novel and its predictable plot arc.

Instead the varied lives and experiences of the translators find themselves against the groundwater of Clarice's own explosive ideas and experimentation, making up a giant engine of language that goes into the translation of her novels. Johnny noted, "My work as a translator makes me think constantly about the limits of a language — the conceptual places English will take you, and the ways in which Portuguese (for example) takes you somewhere else, not exactly the same imaginative or intellectual destinations." As I said to Katrina deep in our conversation about Clarice, grammar is a social construct, and it's much more malleable and fallible than is often perceived. Grammar's mirage of rigidity seems to be what Clarice is most thrilled by deconstructing, allowing her ideas to roam in an open field. Katrina said, "The more you understand Portuguese and the more you understand Clarice, the more you can recognize how she makes her writing feel wrong in a subtle way. Her sentences go against grammar, but the way she writes makes it nevertheless seem right, because of the rhythm and because her very particular idiolect is so compelling."

"She's thrilling to read," Alison said, "and that thrill comes from the combination of her ideas, which are not comfortably housed in language, and the way language has to work to keep up with her. And she does have strange turns of phrase, which make you stop and think about what she's saying." This awareness of language's limits, or perhaps language breaking at the seams to express Clarice's ideas, has a history of being subdued in previous translations, so that its oddness didn't feel like a by-product of translation. Idra noted, "Working with her sentences, I could see how many layers they had. How they could be straightforward and also have the sense of surging questions underneath. She's so good at creating a sentence that is technically straightforward while reading it feels almost mythical." With a more global world in the last 50 years, the style of translation has also changed. The idea of an uncomfortable reader, or perhaps a reader who is simply aware that a text shouldn't be changed for their own comfort, is more acceptable. Likewise, there is the expectation of feeling like an outsider when reading translation, of being temporarily confused, or for the syntax to still feel "foreign." This new approach to translation has created a space to embrace Clarice's distinctive play with language.

Alison spoke of this stylistic change, saying, "If the language is strange, it's strange for a reason. I like to think about what it does to the reader in Portuguese and how that can be replicated for an English reader. What is she trying to do, and how can I do that too? And just let her be herself." Alison noted that Clarice uses verbs in a strange way, saying, "She'll say, so-and-so 'dilated their eyes,' but you open your eyes, and you dilate your pupils. That strangeness carries across into English perfectly, as long as you don't use a more conventional verb. In the process of interpreting something, you might unconsciously correct things that sound odd. You have to be careful not to let those 'corrections' flow through into the translation." Part of the change in the approach was to let Clarice sound both like her strange-self but also like her Brazilian-self, who wrote in Portuguese. In English translations, her syntax is characteristically strange in addition to being stylistically Portuguese, instead of being Americanized or made to feel like it was originally written in English.

The more the translators spoke about the complexities of translation, and often what is lost during the act, my mind drifted in a different direction. Instead of looking toward the translators' creativity and ingenuity in finding alternatives, I kept returning again and again to their own journeys into Brazil, into Rio, into Portuguese to better understand Clarice in her original words. Collectively, they'd worked so hard to understand, to get close to her. Having read so much Clarice, translated by such a myriad of translators, her voice had always felt singular, pulsating through the texts. Still, how did the Clarice I'd read in translation hold up to Clarice in the original Portuguese?

Unlike Katrina and Idra, my first Clarice novel was not *The Passion According to G.H.*, but instead *The Hour of the Star*, published in October 1977, less than two months before Clarice's death. I have this in common with Magdalena, who told me she had just graduated from Harvard and was teaching in Santiago when she

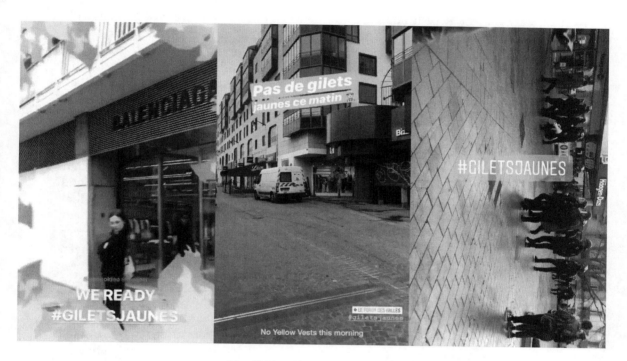

Mona Varichon, *23 mars 2019 Gilets Jaunes Acte XIX*, 2020, HD video, color, stereo sound, 11:23 min.

first read Clarice in the form of Giovanni Pontiero's translation of *The Hour of the Star*. For myself, it was Benjamin Moser's 2011 translation, which I came across a few years post-grad while I was volunteering in a used bookstore, similar to how Johnny first found Clarice. My brain felt immediately electrified by the ideas coursing through the novel. I shrieked out loud — *Clarice!* — reading on the New York City subway at rush hour, bringing everyone's attention to me while my head was still deep in the book. Later, when I was reading *Água Viva*, I wrote to a friend. I told him that riding my bike in the November cold over the Williamsburg Bridge, after going over the bridge's peak and starting to speed up as the decline increased, is almost exactly the same feeling one can receive from reading a single sentence of Clarice Lispector.

In *The Hour of the Star*, Clarice's surrogate writer, Rodrigo S.M., integrates his own practice for the first quarter of the novel, as he obsesses over writing about a singular character — the girl Macabéa. Aware of the multiplicity of ideas within the writing, Rodrigo S.M. tells the reader early on, "I do not intend for what I'm about to write to be complex, though I'll have to use the words that sustain you." This concept of language bending and breaking norms to match a rush of ideas is characteristic of Clarice, part of her pull as a writer. Magdalena said, "As I read the story of Macabéa the typist and Rodrigo S.M. the writer, as framed by Clarice Lispector in her author's dedication, my spirit and heart and brain were exploding. I had no idea language could be used in such a way." Magdalena learned Portuguese when she started a PhD program at UCLA, where she studied with Elizabeth Marchant, who taught a class exclusively devoted to Clarice.

Magdalena reread *The Hour of the Star*, now in Marchant's class and in the original Portuguese. She told me, "My brain, spirit, and heart exploded all over again."

It was Magdalena who was able to speak to the beauty of translation's sacrificial nature: "Translation requires me to embrace both loss and difference. The loss of never fully being able to experience Clarice in all the languages I do not know, and the loss of not being able to read the majority of the world's writing in the original language." Yes, translations are different versions which omit or replace or attempt to replicate, which lose the original rhythm and word associations, but more than that the translations are in many ways deeply personal readings of Clarice's beautifully strange, variegated texts. These readings are intimate by nature, representing years of scholarship and each translators' own spiritual transformation. Magdalena mentions, "With every translation comes a new and different path toward the spirit of the original text. This is beautiful and exciting."

Each of the translators have been through their own G.H.-like metamorphosis, arriving at their own relationship and understanding of the texts. Instead of her 2010s translation being presented by all one translator, offering a unified reading of Clarice, a web of multiple readings emerges instead. Each novel offers a glimpse into each translator's own unique discovery of Clarice's meaning. "Rereading her work today," said Magdalena, "in whatever language, is a meditation in everything it means to be human in a cosmos that is much bigger than us." As a reader, it's a unique gift to receive, which for many of the translators has taken a lifetime to assemble. It's a gift I'm not so sure my soul could ever be ready to truly begin to accept.

Poets Writing Prose

From

Seagull BOOKS

A Calm Fire

and Other Travel Writings

Philippe Jaccottet

Translated by John Taylor

"A highly erudite mêlée of memoir, meditation, and criticism."
—*Times Literary Supplement*

The Swiss List
Cloth $27.50

Patches of Sunlight, Or of Shadow

Safeguarded Notes, 1952–2005

Philippe Jaccottet

Translated by John Taylor

"Jaccottet's work is rooted in a deep and sustained reflection on the existential reality of death, and the countervailing abundance of life, and a reading of nature and culture through that lens."—*On the Seawall*

The Swiss List
Cloth $27.50

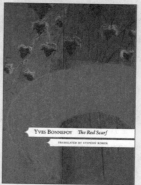

The Red Scarf

Followed by "Two Stages" and Additional Notes

Yves Bonnefoy

Translated and with an Afterword by Stephen Romer

"With *The Red Scarf*, Bonnefoy makes a breach in the past. But there is nothing merely nostalgic in this magisterial autobiographical essay."
—*Le Monde*

The French List
Cloth $24.50

Rome, 1630

The Horizon of the Early Baroque, Followed by Five Essays on Seventeenth-Century Art

Yves Bonnefoy

Edited, Translated, and with a Afterword by Hoyt Rogers

A richly illustrated account by the late French poet of Rome at one of its greatest moments: the baroque high point of 1630.

The French List
Cloth $45.00

Distributed by the University of Chicago Press   www.press.uchicago.edu

Mona Varichon, *Échauffement pour Air*, 2020 (in collaboration with Nicolas Faubert & Jacob Eisenmann), HD video, color, stereo sound, 25:17 min. This video, commissioned by the Cité Internationale des Arts as a dialogue between resident artists and curators, follows Cité residents as they travel through Paris to different Cité locations, dancing and chatting about funerals and Leonardo Da Vinci while in an auditorium, on the subway, on the Pont Louis Philippe and in the unruly gardens of Montmartre.

THE CAVE
MICHAEL TORRES

In my truck, I'm the only person in the parking lot.
Across from me, a gathering of what sounds like
friends outside a Catholic outreach center that advertises

free BBQ, root beer, and a taste of salvation on Friday nights.
I'm reading a book under the light pole's shine in the center
of the lot. The window halfway down, light strikes a thin

shadow across my pages. Tomorrow afternoon, my daughter
will be born. Right now, through the window I hear someone
laugh, say, "No way." Further out, there's a storm. Lightning

bolts desire sky. The rain will either arrive or miss me entirely
and I can't decide which will help promote the best version
of myself. I listen for thunder but catch only a few words

from the maybe-Catholics. Then, the smell of charcoal. More
laughter after that. Another car pulls into a spot near me. A man,
younger than me, gets out and takes a skateboard from his backseat.

I've closed the book on my lap, though I haven't noticed yet.
The younger man locks the car and rides away on the skateboard.
I stare, ride away with him. There's a breeze then,

and what the breeze carries.

And what made me think of you,

Mona Varichon, *And What Made Me Think Of You*, 2016, HD video, color, stereo sound, 10:00 min. Reached over the phone, the artist's mother gets ready for work while describing streets, phantom limbs, bygone vineyards, and native butterfly trees that recently reminded her of her daughter.

NOSTALGIA FOR NOSTALGIA: BTS ON AMERICAN TV

MICHELLE CHO

Nostalgia is ubiquitous in late capitalism. In both its spatial and temporal modes of homesickness and a longing for the past, nostalgia can be a response to uncertainty, a longing for comfort in dark times. Nostalgia signifies the impossible desire for return, whether we figure this as prenatal plenitude, the exile's lost homeland, or the putative completeness of the couple form: 1+1=1. Specifically in the context of American politics today, we see many competing versions. There's the poisonous revanchism of the Trump cult, which filters the 1950s through a tacky '80s tabloid brand. Biden's Build Back Better is also a nostalgic vision, but one that takes us to different post-crisis moments, telescoping the Great Depression and the Great Recession.

Today's more wide-ranging pop nostalgic aesthetics emerge from a planetary crisis that makes looking *ahead* a problem. But they also have to contend with the growing acknowledgment that the past — especially the romanticized Cold War '50s — was demonstrably unlivable for many, whose newly audible voices claim humanity in the present. What's known about that putative golden age of postwar prosperity that was beamed around the world through pop music, Hollywood film, and, especially television, is that it was an Eden for a select few. No, nostalgia either for the '50s or the '80s is monstrous and uncanny. And yet, the iconography of Americana that saturated popular media throughout the Cold War maintains its affective force. Today's nostalgia struggles to contain the impolitic longing for McLuhan's fantasized global village of the mid-20th century, but perhaps it also does something else.

What's ironic about the present is that many of us are homesick and also sick of being at home. Our melancholy knows no bounds. So many are also literally displaced, unhoused, unable to imagine comfort, adding another layer of impossibility that makes our current nostalgia different from prior pop culture versions we've cycled through during the last half century. What's abundantly clear is that nostalgia (for the '50s sifted through the '80s or the '30s through the aughts) is an argument about the past, not necessarily as a set of disputed historical facts but as an affective force and aspirational ideal. We see this in the completeness with which nostalgia permeates the fashion and media aesthetics of the current moment, especially pop music. As Billboard watchers note, 2020's biggest acts all deployed nostalgic pop aesthetics to fashion the sounds of the year,

from Lady Gaga and Ariana Grande's '90s diva reboot to The Weeknd's '80s technopop to Dua Lipa's disco-revival in her Grammy-nominated album *Future Nostalgia*. But, how do we make sense of a trend that's also so enduring as to be a classic feature of mass media?

Arguably, no musical group is more central to this zeitgeist than the Korean pop band BTS, whose televised performances — including the recent Grammys spectacular — are ultra-mediated paeans to nostalgia. The group and its large, international fandom routinely make headlines, sometimes standing in for the entirety of Gen Z, even though the BTS ARMY (the group's official fandom) is far more diverse in age, gender, race, and nationality than most observers recognize. While the group has had a foothold on American pop charts for several years, their visibility reached a new apex in 2020, with three number-one hit singles. There's an atavistic prestige to truly mass-cultural stardom, and BTS now garners breathless praise (rather than racist microaggressions) from mainstream journalists. Outlets like *Time*, *Esquire*, *Variety*, and even *WSJ Magazine* have boarded the bandwagon, aiming to explain for the umpteenth time the "it" factor that makes the group simultaneously edgy and approachable, while selling to the group's reliable stan army. The key to BTS's allure is actually quite simple: the group is subcultural because of its foreignness, but its crossover success in the US owes to the group's singular focus on remixing familiar genres and narratives of American pop music and entertainment. Despite their cancelled 2020 world tour, the group has been *more* visible in American mass media in the last year than ever before, to repeatedly make the case for their convincing crossover into the US mainstream pop landscape via coverage in legacy media outlets. The latter seek better cross-platform integration (e.g., network TV on YouTube) by capitalizing on the group's passionate, massive, and "very online" fandom.

Live, televised performance has been the engine of BTS's crossover, at least in the testimony of many BTS converts, and their television strategy harkens back to earlier eras of American entertainment spectacle pioneered by vaudeville and, later, television variety shows.

The group's charm offensive across the big three networks has been thorough, scoring high profile guests spots on Corden and Colbert (CBS), Fallon (NBC), Kimmel (ABC), *SNL* (NBC), and *Good Morning America* (ABC), today's heirs of 20th-century variety show formats. The group has also performed on every televised music show in the US media market: the American Music Awards, the Billboard Music Awards, the MTV Video Music Awards, and the Grammys. In the latter case, BTS first appeared as special guests during Lil Nas X's performance of his 2019 hit "Old Town Road," rather than performing their own music and choreography. On the 2021 show, BTS got a stand-alone, remote performance, despite being passed over for an award. Hence, recognition from the Recording Academy as music professionals, rather than television eye candy, remains the group's Everest.

Highlighting technical mastery and intertextual aesthetics, these televised performances present a somewhat contradictory appeal to viewers, eschewing the media strategy of their Anglo-American contemporaries who aim instead for radio play and platform ubiquity on Spotify or iTunes. Instead, BTS lean into their polished performance repertoire, despite the risk of reinforcing the image of K-pop that supports the racist view of Asian bodies as robotic, unassimilable, perpetually foreign. Precisely by exporting the conventions of the South Korean pop industry, which closely integrates lavishly produced TV performances with music marketing and promotion, the group also dominates all manner of digital platforms. Like other K-pop acts, BTS match eye-popping group choreography to their musical tracks, displaying star-levels of charisma and athletic coordination in each televised musical number, while focusing parasocial intimacy on social media and in offstage media content. This duality appeals to almost everyone, except for a certain sort of straight, white, middle-aged audience, in whom BTS tends to produce intense xenophobia. (In only the most recent version of this phobic reaction, a German radio host called BTS a virus akin to COVID-19.) This group, however, belongs to the demographic for whom a lot of late-night network television is written. Notably, BTS has been a repeat guest only on Fallon and Corden, whose shows emphasize pop musicality and playful, millennial energy. Alyxandra Vesey details this strategy in a 2015 essay in *The Spectator* — "Working for @LateNightJimmy."

As Benjamin M. Han details in *Beyond the Black and White TV: Asian and Latin American Spectacle in Cold War America*, variety television of the 1950s–'70s frequently featured "ethnic spectacle" — musical performances by Asian and Latinx performers — to assert an ideology of globalism for an imagined overseas audience. This was part of a broader trend in commercial television to produce an anticommunist, multicultural vision of America, and circulate it through popular music and entertainment spectacle. The strategy aligned with attempts to mitigate Soviet criticisms of US anti-Black racism, on vivid display in the Civil Rights struggle, with State Department–funded tours that sent artists like Louis Armstrong and Dizzy Gillespie around the world as "jazz ambassadors." While the function of diversity in musical performance on television no longer hews to Cold War dualism, late night still seems to govern the Overton window of what counts as part of a national zeitgeist, which BTS's American reception makes clear. If Kimmel retains vaudeville's ethnic sidekick — notably, when BTS appeared on his show in 2017, the group shared language lessons with parking-lot security guard turned regular cast member Guillermo Rodriguez — Jimmy Fallon revises midcentury, variety-show cultural politics by highlighting the iconoclasm of foreign language musical performers on his show.

Despite truisms about the power of pop music to transcend cultural and linguistic barriers, television's spectacular function remains a keystone of BTS's publicity strategy because the group gets limited radio play for their Korean-language tracks — the lion's share of their output. Their sole track sung entirely in English is last summer's shimmery, retro, disco-pop hit, "Dynamite." The song's overt superficiality and its outlier status in the group's discography laid bare the xenophobia of US music industry gatekeepers, as it became their first track to hit the elusive number-one spot on the Billboard Hot 100 singles chart, in no small part because it was the first of BTS's songs to receive substantial radio play. However, the group's subsequent, Korean-language

single "Life Goes On" also rose to the top spot, despite its near total exclusion from radio airwaves in the United States, a testament to the steady growth of their fandom, whose ARMY acronym, despite its martial connotations, stands for "Adorable Representative MC for Youth." There's a term for a BTS fan who discovered the group during COVID-19: "Pandemic ARMY," and ARMY's ranks are expanding apace of the group's prolific transmedia engagement.

Seen in this light, the televised performance of "Dynamite" on Corden's show from late 2020 takes on a sharpened significance as a retort to the era of American cultural imperialism via "global TV" — the image of America used as propaganda during the '50s expansion of television infrastructure in the Pacific, detailed by media historian James Schwoch in *Global TV: New Media and the Cold War, 1946-69*. BTS exit a trailer, dance their way across the tarmac, board a jet in first class, and deplane straight onto a simulacrum of Corden's L.A. studio stage, topped by its *Late Late Show* marquee. The final segment of the performance takes place on a copy of the interview set, complete with piped-in sounds of a faux-studio audience. The only element that can't be fabricated is, of course, Corden himself, who remains absent from the scene. Instead, the famously hammy group member Jimin takes a seat in James's chair behind his interview desk, before joining the rest of the members for the song's closing bars as they add a realist touch — the staple, awkward musical-interlude shuffle. "Dynamite" is a simulacrum of American pop, exported and sold around the world, so it's fitting that the performance would stage the group's most commercial track as a virtual movement of cargo via trailer/shipping container

While looking at the image,
you think of what is missing.

Mona Varichon, *No, I Was Thinking Of Life (CC)*, 2018, HD video, color, stereo sound, 12:00 min loop. Made from a series of recorded phone calls between the artist and her mother Malak El Zanaty Varichon, this film spans impassioned discussions about Jonas Mekas, funerals and improvisation.

from Seoul to Los Angeles. But the performance also, again, cites American midcentury variety television, which often used the trope of tourist mobility in special episodes shot abroad or segments that simulated international flights when air travel for most Americans offered a fantasy of glamour and luxury, rather than the ignominies of sardine-can seating arrangements and endless security lines.

While the performance dematerializes the Pacific Ocean expanse that separates Seoul and Los Angeles, it nonetheless affirms the significance of place — it is important that we know that BTS travel via Incheon International Airport on their nation's flagship carrier Korean Air. As the group transforms what is possible in the realm of mediated live performance on American TV, BTS also draws attention to the difference place makes, even, or especially, in the realm of remote content creation under pandemic constraints. In the jumbled collage of Americana that is their "Dynamite" music video, BTS deploys a series of nostalgic locations that mashup millennial pop culture's midcentury clichés: the teenager's bedroom, the donut shop/diner, the record store, plus a roller-rink-turned-discotheque. There's also a '90s *Space Jam* segment on a basketball court and a *Teletubbies*-inspired chorus. What may seem like mere postmodern monstrosity is actually a commentary on the pleasures and perils of nostalgia as well as a subtle nod to the racial history of the pop crossover.

BTS was nominated for their first Grammy in the category of "Best Pop Duo/Group Performance," not for their 2020 magnum opus *Map of the Soul: 7*, a genre-experimenting LP that offered a career-culminating statement on their seven-year history. Instead, their nomination was for "Dynamite," which was chosen by their US distributor Columbia Records specifically to engineer a crossover hit. In addition to the comfortingly pastel sets, the group choreography is also surprisingly familiar. Throughout the music video, the group spells out its debt to the King of Pop and first crossover teen idol sensation Michael Jackson by moonwalking across the set. However, the influence of MJ's *televisual* presence only becomes clear when comparing the movements of the "Dynamite" choreography with Jackson's famed live performance of "Billie Jean" on the 1983 TV special *Motown 25: Yesterday, Today, Forever*, where he first debuted the moonwalk. Highlighting MJ's stylized miming of the '50s greaser combing his hair, the dance moves in "Dynamite" place BTS in a genealogy of crossover musicians, deliberately pointing to American pop's history of deracination.

As Michael D. Dwyer notes in *Back to the Fifties: Nostalgia, Hollywood Film, and Popular Music of the Seventies and Eighties*, Michael Jackson repeatedly appealed to '50s teen idol culture to accomplish his crossover from Motown phenom to mainstream pop star, specifically operationalizing the music video form, despite its explicitly anti-Black MTV platform. What endures across the pop culture landscape is the way that a pre–Civil Rights image of Americana secures mainstream pop as invisibly racialized. In other words, what's undeniable to us now — the *whiteness* of Reagan-era nostalgia — was indeed what passed as American culture writ large, both at home and, importantly, in the many overseas markets in which American popular culture circulated. Framing the question of pop nostalgia transnationally necessarily changes the way we read nostalgia's rhetorical gestures, as they signify differently to geographically distinct audiences, a point largely missed by the pop industry gatekeepers at the Recording Academy. BTS headlined the roster of remote performances for the 63rd Grammy Awards. Incidentally, the show was newly helmed by producer Ben Winston, who co-created "Carpool Karaoke" when he worked on *The Late Late Show with James Corden* and tweeted admiration for the Corden performance I've been writing about here.

BTS's Grammy aspirations have a crucial context that goes beyond thirst for recognition from US pop industry peers. They've been running up against a hard deadline: their mandatory conscription in South Korea's military, which is one of the many enduring traces of the Cold War that remain in South Korean society. BTS's oldest member was due to enlist on his 28th birthday on December 4, 2020, which would have required the group to reshuffle the seven-member lineup to which fans are deeply attached. South Korea's National Assembly came to the rescue in the nick of time, notably, after BTS received their Grammy nomination, passing a revision to the Military Service Act to grant a two-year deferral for high-profile pop musicians, so that Jin could remain a BTS member through the other side of the pandemic. This deferral provision is being called the "BTS Law" in South Korea.

BTS's use of the old-school medium of network television and its integration of music performance as mainstream entertainment keeps alive a notion of a broad global public, codified during the Cold War, that's been lost with audience fragmentation and narrow-casting. This suggests that the key modifier of globalism today is its virtuality, a point that is also old school — harking back to a mid-20th-century vision of fantasized mobility — at the same time that it responds to the relentlessly material crises of the present moment. The group's large, international fandom exceeds the scope of the United States, but so does American television's reach and its aspirations to the universality of its bourgeois-liberal (and in the case of late-night TV, often blatantly patriarchal) world horizons. While there are other examples of televised pop music performances with comparable aims to broad public reception — e.g., the Super Bowl half-time show — BTS's targeted conquest of American TV viewership is a throwback to an older model of networked televisual connection, but in a moment in which such connections signify different boundaries and geopolitical dynamics. Mainstreaming foreign languages in mass media and decentering US players is important, even if the forms on offer are reassuringly familiar, and BTS are meaningfully disruptive in their language of expression and their provenance, outside the circuits of Euro-American pop industries.

The outright falsification of US democratic ideals during the Trump era coincided exactly with the meteoric rise of BTS's popularity, as well as K-pop's visibility as a genre of popular entertainment in North America. In this context, while BTS's US television appearances are made possible through the group's strategic deployment of nostalgia, they also draw our attention to the difference that inheres in repetition. BTS's exceptional presence and mediating function reminds us that no matter how homesick, you can't go home again.

Brontez Purnell, still from *Free Jazz*, 2013, 8 mm film. Performed by Brontez Purnell Dance Company.

THE THING ON THE PHONE

STEPHEN MARCHE

This story was written with the aid of Sudowrite, using GPT-3 from OpenAI in beta, February 2021. The buttons included "Wormhole," "Twist," "Character," and "Description." All were used at least once. The text is 17.1 percent computer-generated. This is a work of fiction. Any resemblance to any person, living or dead, is coincidental.

No one believed that the governor of the Bank of England resigned "to spend more time with his family." Who could believe that line? In the absence of any meaningful explanation, the internet generated theories with its usual squalid logic. He must have had a falling out with the prime minister, or he had been trying to sabotage Brexit, or an old City scandal had cropped up, or, drifting further into the conspiratorial back alleys of the network, he belonged to a pedophile ring, or the Jewish illuminati, or an intergalactic treaty organization. But the departure of Mark Chair from the Bank of England was the rare case of the cover story being real. He did quit his role as governor to spend more time with his family. He left the Bank of England because his daughter Chloe was expelled from school for biting a teacher.

When Chair showed up at the school, canceling a lecture on macroprudential policy he was to deliver at the Council on Foreign Relations, furious to be disturbed by such a trivial matter as a school biting incident, the headmistress didn't argue. She didn't say anything. A slender woman in her mid-40s, dressed in a dark dress and shoes with high heels, her cool composure belied the edge of rage that showed in her eyes. She took out an iPad and opened a tab.

At first Chair didn't know what he was looking at. White and red and yellow blobs. Almost abstract. It was a thumb. It was the flesh of a thumb. Flesh exposed all the way, maybe half a centimeter of bone showing. Chloe had nearly bitten it off.

As they drove out of the school grounds, Mark and Chloe Chair looked like any other wealthy and powerful father and daughter.

"We better go to the Old Place, Prowl," Chair told his driver. Prowl's first name was Bill, but everybody called him Prowl.

"Wales?"

"I'm afraid so."

The Old Place in Wales, Plas Hen, was remote, an old Georgian mansion that had once served as a country hotel. Chair had insisted on the property when accepting the position as governor of the Bank, a secure place where the family could weekend. It was a long drive to Plas Hen but in London there would be press. There would be questions.

"My youngest bit some teacher and they're making a big deal out of it," Chair told Prowl, as a sort of explanation.

Prowl nodded sagely. "My father always said that children are the enemy."

Mark snorted. "What does that make you?"

"Well, exactly."

Before he had been governor of the Bank of England, Mark Chair had been governor of the Bank of Canada, and before that, senior executive at Goldman Sachs, and before that a Rhodes Scholar, and before that the son of an Anglican minister in Fort Smith, in the Northwest Territories. He had traveled, over the course of a lifetime of achievement, from the ultimate nowhere to the heart of power, admired by conservatives and liberals, by presidents and his drivers. To the internet, he was just an icon of the financial system. To the people who knew him, he was the smartest guy in the room whose sense of calm control could stabilize the economies of whole continents, a man with four loving daughters, a brilliant wife who'd accepted the Nobel Peace Prize on behalf of Médecins Sans Frontières.

Chair was halfway relieved his wife was out of contact. She was not really out of contact. There is no out of contact. She had a satellite phone. She was triaging the victims of a sexual terrorism campaign in the Eastern Congo. A case of phone addiction, even in her own daughter, might seem trivial. Chair and his wife had always tried to share parenting responsibilities equally, but Brexit had consumed him with a never-ending array of crises to negotiate. It was his turn. Chloe was his problem to solve.

The easiest way for parents to excuse a child is to blame themselves. How long since he'd seen his daughter? How long since the last parents' weekend? It couldn't be six weeks. But his wife had attended, he recalled. He'd been in Brussels.

Chloe's hair was shorter than the last time he'd seen her, cropped in an odd curve, like a statue of Joan of Arc, or like a statue in a movie of Joan of Arc anyway. Her eyes didn't seem to blink, and, with a succulent sadness, he remembered her, seven years old again, running over the tundra as they gathered wild blueberries in pails that time they had returned to Canada for a vacation, and there was a time then when she had cut open her own thumb, and they had had to helicopter her into the hospital in Edmonton. She had never been a violent girl, only serious and private. He would have liked to cover her with a blanket. He desired to feed her thick soup and buttered bread.

His phone buzzed and he checked it automatically. It was his eldest daughter Abby, studying artificial intelligence at Stanford. She texted:

—The Simulation revealed!

She linked to a story on a conspiracy theory website which argued, from the assumption that the entire world was a giant simulation created by future engineers to preserve a memory of their ancestors, that he, Mark Chair, was a "downloaded consciousness" put there by the engineers as a "simulation manager."

—so dad confess your the guardian for the simulation aren't you

—lol

—god learn to use an emoji old man

—lmfao. For a Guardian of the Simulation I'm not very tech savvy.

A shiver of self-blame licked his spine. He was always on his phone. The children of alcoholics learn that the bottle matters more than they do. The new children were learning that the phone comes first. Chloe had learned.

Behind the rush of guilt followed a pang to dampen its force. Chloe had always been apart, more articulate than her sisters but less understood. He and his wife had discussed whether she was a genius.

"What are you looking at on your phone?" he asked.

"A thing."

"What thing are you looking at?"

"The thing on the phone."

"Chloe, this is serious. You just were expelled from a school you told us you loved. Put away your phone so we can talk."

"We can talk while I'm looking at the thing on my phone."

"We can't. I can't."

Chloe shrugged. Chair reached over to take the phone physically out of her hand, pulled it back in sharp pain. A cut squeezed blood out on his thumb. It was red and irregular, a gash opening up into a wound. He sucked the iron-scarlet off his knuckle. Prowl, in the rear-view mirror, queried with his eyes.

"I need the thing on my phone," Chloe said.

Four hours later, the Mercedes pulled into the long drive through the woods up to the Old Place. The gray stones of its foundation were rough, craggy, and weathered. The roof was slate, gray, and soft to the touch. White paint was peeling away in patches. Black shutters framed the windows.

The Old Place stood in the woods at the end of a long drive, the trees surrounding it, their branches rustling in the spring and summer breeze made the place seem like it was in a vast wilderness, part of the wilderness.

Chloe unplugged her phone, and without taking her eyes off the screen, headed straight to the back of the house where she knew a latch into the coal room was always open. She was out of sight before Chair managed to stand out of the car.

Prowl, lifting their winter coats out of the trunk, was watching her go.

"Teenagers and their phones," he muttered cheerfully.

Chloe had taken the big chair in the library. It was closest to the power outlet. The chair had a scent of old leather, dried lavender, and dusty books.

"Chloe, I'm going to take your phone away now, just so we can talk."

No response registered on his daughter's face. He approached, reached out his hand, then found himself twisted on the ground behind the chair.

The pain had been sharp. The confusion crackled. He possessed no memory of what she'd done to throw him.

Prowl entered the room with a working-class smile on his face. The governor of the Bank of England had been tossed like a bag of onions by a little girl with her knees crooked under her legs like a Zed.

"Need a hand, sir?" His voice was a companionable rumble.

"I need something."

Prowl strode his cockney bouncer self up to the girl and her hand shot straight out, like a rod, into his solar plexus. Prowl stood, crouched, frozen like a defragging screen, and the big man crumbled, panting.

One of the twins had left a hockey helmet in an upstairs bedroom. Chloe allowed the helmet over her head. Prowl brought rope from the shed. They strung one coil around her shins and another around her chest. She allowed them to fasten the ropes and then tighten them. Her eyes, the entire time, never wavered from the phone. Then Chair slapped the phone out of her hands. Chloe passed out like a flipped switch.

"Nice one" Prowl said.

The governor considered, sighing. "I have faith that there are solutions."

It was dark, Chair saw. He had not seen the dark set on. He was sweating. He hadn't noticed himself starting to sweat.

"Go bury it," he said, handing the phone to Prowl. It was an old model, an iPhone 4, practically a museum piece. He took out the SIM card and folded it in four. Chloe moaned in her sleep. "Cover it with leaves after so you can't seen where it is."

His actions had already diverged from any action he could justify. A large English man was burying his daughter's phone in the Welsh rook-filled woods the way you might bury a bird that had flown into a window for the sake of tender-hearted child.

The Old Place was a quiet analog zone, with a cupboard of old board games and shelves filled with rotting tomes of 1940s medical texts and 1880s Methodist tracts and the most popular novels of every decade, long forgotten, and 79 acres of thick woods attached. On its edge was a paleolithic site, the Crick Stones, which was why the government owned the property.

The druids' uses for the Crick Stones were unknown. In the 19th century, the central stone, which was like a bluestone donut, had become a traditional destination for women who wanted to get pregnant. They passed backward through the Crick Stone seven times. There were Medieval records of women putting children whom they believed to be changelings through it, too. Fairy exchange had become a decent source of tourist revenue for the local town.

Chair woke up to a text from Abby.

—What happened with Glowy?

—She bit a teacher. I'm with her at the Old Place.

—Just for biting?

—How do you know about Chloe already? I just picked her up.

—Margaret McMillian.

An old school friend of Abby's, a few forms below her, one of that roving gang of thuggish upper-class teenage girls his daughter had run with.

—Don't tell Margaret.

—I will keep it off the network.

In the smoky kitchen, Prowl was fixing Chloe eggs and bacon. She smiled at her father when he entered. She and Prowl had been joking.

"I don't know what they've been feeding that girl at her school," Prowl said. "That's the eighth egg she's eaten and I tremble to guess how much bacon."

"A steady diet of lies," Chloe said.

"What's that, miss?"

"A steady diet of lies. That's what they fed me at the school. Well, that's not really true. The term 'lie' implies that they were aware of falsehood. Bad data. They fed me bad data."

Prowl, flummoxed, made an excuse. "Well, it's nice to be on vacation, isn't it?"

Chloe swallowed another fried egg whole. "I suppose you want to take me for a walk," she said to her father.

The Welsh winter was mild that year. The squelch of mud underfoot was satisfactory. The path was coarse and slick. Father and daughter on a family hike — that's what Mark could almost pretend it was. The oaks and holly were thick on that property, but they had clearly been planted, sculpted. The oaks were heavy and smoky. They smelled of rot and decay and a certain musty sweetness. It did not have the breathable relief of old growth forest. There is no wilderness in Europe, just zoos of smaller or larger size.

Chloe walked ahead, rapidly. He had to hurry to keep up.

"You want to talk about what happened at the school?" he asked.

"No."

"We shouldn't talk about it? You don't want to talk about it?"

"No."

"You bit a teacher's thumb nearly off."

"You know I couldn't do that."

"Did somebody tell you to do that?"

She smirked. "That is such an old person thing to say."

"What happened then?"

"The thing on the phone."

"Tell me about the thing on the phone."

"You know, dad, I'm not sure I could even say it in a way that makes sense."

"Try."

The girl gave a sly smile. Its inward curve was identical to the external curve. "I'd have to look it up on the phone."

The Crick Stones appeared on the path in front of them. Chloe ran up in delight to inspect the stone circle at the center, and Mark decided to forget the crisis while they wandered. He told himself that he would wait for the addiction

Brontez Purnell, still from *Free Jazz*, 2013, 8 mm film. Performed by Brontez Purnell Dance Company.

to wear off before a proper confrontation about what she had done. This was the 21st century, and he had money and connections. He would hire experts, experts in phone addiction, experts in gifted children with heightened social anxiety, criminal solicitors.

As they walked back to the house, Chloe turned to her father. "I think I've found a way to tell you."

"Tell me about what?"

"The thing on the phone."

"Tell me."

Chloe cleared her throat. "There is no information to convey," she said. Then her face blanked.

That night, Chair woke from a dream he couldn't remember and saw a faint blue glow at his door, and he followed it down the stairs to the sitting room with the pink wallpaper and the chairs still covered in plastic because he hadn't informed the caretaker he was coming, and there was Chloe, squatting on the floor with an old Blackberry, and on the Blackberry, which she must have rescued from some junk drawer somewhere in the house, the drawer where they kept the obsolete phones. She was watching, on that Blackberry, a surgery, a video, muted, of a surgeon cutting open a thoracic cavity. The surgery was a continuous shot of a man's upper torso, frozen in a contorted position, the skin stretched taut over his ribs and vertebrae. The surgeon was silhouetted against the bright lights behind him, his face indistinguishable.

"Chloe," he said softly. She looked up. She handed over the phone and lay down, fast asleep. He carried his daughter up to bed.

¤

Before he could figure out how she had found the Blackberry, how she had charged it and turned it on and connected it, the prime minister called to discuss the financial instruments surrounding fishing vessels, which would affect the whole sector for the foreseeable future. Chair had no choice. The local pub, the Owl and the Pussycat, gave him the back room for these meetings. The widow who ran the place had family in Canada and slipped him a surreptitious ale with a bite of bread and cheese tucked behind the screen, out of sight. It was all so stupid. They called him to know what the reality was and they hated him for telling them what the reality was. He had to explain to the Brexit negotiators that if British fishermen couldn't finance their vessels through European banks, it would lead to less competition which would lead to more expensive loans on fishing vessels, which would lead to more expensive boats. He hung up knowing that the pointlessness was the point. The populist wave existed to express rage at elites like himself but they still wanted elites like him to solve their problems. They hated being a part of the network that they needed.

He returned to Plas Hen in the late afternoon. Prowl was at the door, leaning over the local taxi, gabbing with the driver.

"She got free," he said. "She has a phone again."

"Prowl, you can't abandon me like this."

"I'm fond of you, governor. I really am. First time I drove, you pulled over at Caffe Nero and picked me up a brew and I knew you were all right. But this is some Northern thing."

"What thing are you talking about?"

Prowl was like a grown man who finds himself frightened by a dark patch of woods off a motorway, gripped by a fear that he might recognize was silly but nonetheless ran deep.

"It's all I can figure. You felt the cold coming off her? I'm not a superstitious man but…"

He lifted up his shirt. The flesh by his ribs was purple and green. They didn't look like bruises so much as pixelated glitches in the flesh.

"It's not you. I don't think it's even her," Prowl said. "I don't know what it is. I don't know what I'm talking about. You do. You will. You're a clever man and you're a good man, too. I have no doubt you'll figure it out. I can't."

"Prowl," Chair pleaded. "Prowl."

Prowl lifted himself delicately into the taxi. "You can keep the phone, governor."

In the kitchen, Chloe sat, sucking her thumb, staring into what must have been Prowl's phone. The tiles were rough and sharp and cold. The walls rose up frosted with dust. She sat sucking her thumb like a five-year-old. She didn't seem to mind that he saw what she was watching. It was pornography, sadomasochistic. The screen showed an ass, being flogged, the flesh shredding off in quivers. It was so pulpy and bloody he couldn't tell if the ass was male or female. She started making a sound. It started out weak, from the rolled-back lips, but it grew into a long wet fluting noise that sounded like some kind of animal in tremendous pain. She was making the noise, and her face was a void. She gasped and made the sound again, and again, the same sound each time, and it rose and fell in intensity, and she didn't seem to notice that he

was there. He wanted to get as far away from the noise as possible, into the forest. He left, quietly, but Chloe never stopped making the noise, and here was the image, projected from the phone, and then again and again and again, the flogged ass, the flayed back, the slow-growing blood-streaked rind.

Chair didn't need Prowl to secure his daughter, it turned out. She allowed him to put on the hockey helmet. She allowed the straps around her shins and forearms. He had to rig up a line so he could winch them at the same time, but he managed. The difficulty was enduring the screaming after he wrested the phone from her hand. Her whinge of denial was the screech of a starving baby, pure animal need.

The tech in the house was relatively easy to destroy. The security services had set him up with a beacon connected to secure government satellites. He went onto the roof and knocked over the beacon. The beacon was smooth and rounded, made of metal and rubber, its top mounted on a two-meter pole. The thing smashed on the flagstones but to be sure, he carted the whole mechanism down to the pond. The beacon slipped through the dry leaves into the stagnant water. The Old Place hadn't had phone lines since the '60s, but Chair believed in thoroughness. He found the main line and snipped it with a pair of garden shears.

Then he had to decide about his own phone. An iPhone X. A pocket full of worldliness. The pull of potentiality. What if the world needed him? What if he needed the world? The police. His wife.

—Did she bite the teacher's thumb?

It was Abby texting him just as he considered tossing his phone into the pond. The water smelled like autumn, brittle leaves rustling in the breeze, the cold crispness of the air, frost pungent.

—How did you know?

—Just something when we were kids.

—?

—Daughter stuff.

—Abby, tell me.

—That summer in Alberta we were all into Simulation Theory.

Mark had always found the simulation theory tiresome. Even clever people, even engineers, had to believe in some nonsense, an alternate world where intelligences other than our own shaped destiny. Everyone needs fairies one way or the other, even if they're pixellated pixies.

—Chloe and the twins believed. I believed.

—What did you all believe?

—The world is a computer simulation, of the past by the future and we're all just code.

—Chloe believes that?

—I don't know. She kept going back and forth even then. Sometimes they believed and sometimes they didn't. You know the North. It's so basic. Those wide fields. That crazy sky. It feels like a computer programme.

—What does this have to do with thumbs?

—The twins thought you couldn't simulate flesh.

—And?

—So they tied Chloe down one day. I wasn't there. They cut open her thumb to see if she was real.

A rustling behind him. Chloe was coming down the flagstone path toward the pond, with the scrunched uncurling of a teenager's face after deep sleep. How she had managed to disentangle herself from the rope and helmet, he did not know.

She sat down beside him. She put her arm around his shoulder.

"You know I see what you're trying to do," she eventually said, laying her head on his arm. "You're trying to stop the thing on the phone."

"What's the thing on the phone?"

"You can't stop it."

"What is it?"

"If you can't even see the thing on the phone, how can you stop it? You can maybe slow it down. You might see its face. You can't stop it. It's coming."

Mark Chair let his daughter hold him, his daughter's little body stronger than his own. She was right. There was a future coming to eat the past, and it would still be hungry. There was nothing anybody could do about it.

There was an unexpected week of calm. Chair hid his phone in an old pickling jar in the cellar, tucked behind a loose stone. They went for long walks and ate huge meals. They visited the fairy stones. They read some of the old ludicrous books that filled the place — an Australian novel from the 1940s about a group of renegade children abandoned in the Outback, a travelogue along the Silk Road by an eccentric noblewoman. If they were a living simulation, they as well delight in its rich detail. Chair tried not to look at his daughter. Like a fish, her lips were cold and cold-blooded, her breath wet and soupy. Her skin white and pale, as if bleached by moonlight.

After a week, Chair, in the middle of the night, rose with a parent's intuition. He knew Chloe wasn't in the house. How he knew he did not know. She wasn't in her bed. She wasn't on the ground. He shouted her name to silence. He opened the door and shouted her name into the woods to silence.

Bill had left the keys to the Mercedes in a basket by the door.

First, he drove to the Crick Stone. He shouted her name into the surrounding woods for half an hour. She wasn't there.

He drove to the town. There was not a light on to investigate. He called her name on the high street to silence. Even though he shouted no lights turned on.

He drove back to the Old Place. He had nowhere else to drive. The cellar was greenly glowing. Chloe was waiting. She had found his phone, and she was lying on the dirt floor in a pool of the glow. The cold in the cellar was extreme, Arctic, murderous.

There was something in her mouth. She let her father reach out and open her lips. She let him open her teeth. It was a thumb in her mouth, a thumb bitten off at the second knuckle, a man's thumb, wet, in the palm of his hand.

He brought the hockey helmet and the straps down to the cellar. He didn't want to risk bringing her up. Chloe didn't look up but in a hoarse voice, said, "This time it's going to be different."

Chair put the helmet on her head. He wrapped the belt around her shoulders. He wrapped the other belt around her shins. "This time I'm going away," his daughter said.

"Is this because of what your sisters did?"

"What did my sisters do?"

"In Alberta. In the North. When they held you down and cut open your thumb."

"You think they were wrong to do that?"

"They were wrong. They were."

"The ancestors want to see how the world worked, wanted to build worlds that work. So here we were. Here we are."

The vertigo of his misunderstanding opened. The rage of his frustrated intelligence seared his temples.

"I don't get it."

"Why do you need to get it?"

His million million questions conveyed into one. "Where are you?"

"Don't worry about me. I'm safe and warm."

"Tell me where you are."

"It would wreck everything if I did."

"Why thumbs then?"

"The thumb is the first digit of the hand. When a person is standing in the medical anatomical position where the palm is facing to the front, the thumb is the outermost digit."

"Why the thumb?"

"The evolution of the fully opposable thumb is usually associated with *Homo habilis*, a forerunner of *Homo sapiens*."

Her little girl's eyes lifted from the phone the slightest crescent. "I used to be so hungry and so cold. Have you ever been so hungry and so cold that your eyes fall apart?"

Chair cinched the belts shut.

"Dad. I'm sorry I made you do all this."

"Stop."

"No. It's good. You did it all for us."

For a flash, he remembered his wife pregnant, Chloe overdue, and her hand pressing up against the inside of the womb. The outline of her hand on the inside of another person. He grabbed his phone. Chloe's eyes shut. She began to shake, her face contorted, agony of transfiguration. She had very long arms, like eels, her armpits as dark and mysterious as sea urchins.

"I'm sorry you have to hurt," she said.

Chair closed the cellar door and bolted it, then ran upstairs as the sound began, a banshee modem screech. The pounding on the walls began, and he took the kettle from the stove and poured hot water over the phone. A magnificent peal of relief tolled over the governor, the relief of powerlessness, of disconnection, and Chloe screamed, in a scream that desired to shred the world and all its meanings.

Chloe screamed for a while, and then she was silent. Mark sat on the floor and listened for her breathing, but he couldn't hear anything at all. She was just an absence in the house.

The internet conjured its usual rush of empty significance from the events at Plas Hen. The police had found the youngest daughter of the governor of the Bank of England dead in a cellar in Wales with her thumbs bitten off. A Reddit community quickly developed: /plashentheory. QAnon believers convinced themselves Chloe's death was connected to the pedophile ring at Comet Pizza in Washington. Simulation believers concocted elaborate fantasies of glitches in the network. Fairy believers claimed Chloe had been changed at the Crick Stone. A few months later, a podcaster with Pushkin Industries did a 12-part series, *The Lonely Death of Chloe Chair*. It had episodes on phone addiction, on cannibalism fetishes, on pica.

There was no lack of information or explanation. You would have to go deep in your search, all the way to the local territories' report, to find out that Mark Chair had moved back to Fort Smith, as close as he could bring himself to the end of the world and the beginning of himself.

Brontez Purnell, still from *Free Jazz*, 2013, 8 mm film. Performed by Brontez Purnell Dance Company.

RE-IMAGING

LEAH UMANSKY

/1/

It's hard to believe in something, whether it's love or hope.

/2/

Not everything in the old world, the before-world, the shadow-world of passed days is null and void.

/3/

Risk and uncertainty are two of the same and it is all about mindset.

/4/

A friend asks, *do you dream in the old world or the new world?* I can't answer. I don't know.

/5/

When does it stop? When does the beauty out itself in the face of fear? Can you see the re-opening? The re-imaging? What will it be like?

/6/

We pivot and pivot and pivot and eventually lift our faces to trace the sun with our eyes. It is a different sorrow – one relishing in heat – but then we stare up at the golden and are kept, held.

It is a petal we trace with our forefinger; its softness is at once visceral – like memory.

/7/

We know what that life was.

We know what this life *is.*

TOO MUCH SALT IS LETHAL

ABRAHAM LIEBERMAN

I. Brownsville, Brooklyn, 1920s

My family settled in Brownsville in South East Brooklyn. It was not chic then and it is not now, but it was not as crowded as the Lower East Side of Manhattan. There were trees, grass, and an elevated train that took you to Manhattan and the Garment Center. Here most Brownsvillers — Jews who had escaped from the czar, the Bolsheviks, or Hitler — worked. From the 1900s to the 1940s, Brownsville grew and to accommodate the newcomers apartment buildings, tenements, five stories high, without elevators, replaced many of the single- and two-family homes.

My aunt Rebecca, one of the six Lieberman children, was born in 1900. She was a big-boned woman, five feet, eight inches tall with a perfectly oval face, cat-like slanted eyes, and high cheek-bones — "genetic gifts" from a 13th-century Mongol invader. Her hair was dark red and long. She came to America with her husband in December 1918, a month after the Armistice that end-ed World War I. After she arrived, she wished she had not come.

"In 1919, six months after we arrived," she said, "my husband died from Flu. In Leningrad, in Moscow, in Kyiv, where people live like rats, they died from Flu. But we lived in the country, in a small vil-lage, where we had no Flu."

Without a husband, or a job, speak-ing Russian, Polish, Yiddish, and some English, Rebecca was desperate. She moved in with her parents, my grandpar-ents. One day later, accompanied by my uncle Louie, she went looking for work.

The economic center of Brownsville was Saratoga Avenue where it crossed Pitkin Avenue. Here were the fine men's clothing stores, the Savile Row of Brooklyn, where people as far away as Long Island, New Jersey, and Westchester came to shop. Here were savings and commercial banks, accountants, and law-yers. Plenty of work — for men. On the other end of Saratoga Avenue was an-other center, hidden in the shadows of the elevated trains. Here five and a half days a week, 50,000 Brownsvillers pushed into rattling cars and rode north and west to Wall Street and the Garment Center. Here was work for everyone: men, wom-en, boys, and girls. Not jobs to have left Russia for — but jobs.

On the northwest corner where the elevated tracks intersect Saratoga Avenue was a diner open from 6:00 a.m. to 4:00 p.m. Next to it was the Ambassador Theatre showing first-run films: *Gone*

with the Wind, *King Kong*, *Casablanca*, and the Marx brothers in *A Day at the Races* and *A Night at the Opera*. Rebecca did not much care for them. On the southeast corner was the People's Cinema showing socialist films: *The Battleship Potemkin*, *Alexander Nevsky*, *City Lights*, and *Modern Times*. Rebecca, when she could, frequent-ed the People's Cinema. Ninety percent of Brownsville voted Democrat, and 90 percent of them, if they could, would have voted Socialist. Both theaters were open from noon to 8:00 p.m. On the southwest corner was a vacant lot — waiting to be built on.

II. Murder, Inc.

On the northeast corner, next to a can-dy store, was a newsstand. It was waiting for Rebecca. All she had to do was raise the cash, no checks — please, buy out the lease, and pay a rental based on a percent of her sales. The previous owner had not fully understood the terms of the lease nor the nature of the men with whom he was dealing. He was later found in New Jersey — in a swamp. The police said he com-mitted suicide by shooting himself twice in the head: one bullet destroyed the vital centers in his brain stem: breathing, heart rate, and movement. The other bullet de-stroyed his cerebellum, his coordination center, which no longer worked without his brain stem.

The three Shapiro brothers, freelance gangsters, ran Brownsville in the 1920s and early 1930s. In the 1930s, a new gang appeared and asked for a "piece of the action." The Shapiros made the mistake of refusing. They thought Abe Reles and his gang were, like them, freelancers; they were not, they were part of an organized crime ring, the Mob. The Shapiros were hunted down, murdered, and replaced by Reles, who, recognizing the power of organization, joined the Mob, becoming its contract killers — "Murder, Inc." From 1931 till 1941, all of the major "hit jobs" (professional killings) in New York and New Jersey were done by Murder, Inc.

Abe Reles was the King of Murder, Inc. and, by extension, King of Brownsville. Abe Reles and Murder, Inc. in turn, were licensed by the Mob to extort Brooklyn businesses such as wholesale bakeries, small manufacturers, trucking fleets, and clothing stores and to install slot machines, card tables, dice games, and betting parlors in poolrooms and candy stores. Murder, Inc. licensed their own "bankers," loan sharks, who charged 20 percent interest per week. You could get a better rate from the banks on the Pitkin Avenue end of Saratoga, except these banks would not lend you $100 ($1,000 in today's currency) to bet on the third race at Belmont Park or the first game of a New York Giants–New York Yankees World Series. An average Murder, Inc. "loan" returned a 120 percent profit to Abe and "the boys." This was a better return, on average, than the Stock Market before it crashed in 1929.

You did not get the chance to operate a Brownsville newsstand by reading the classified ads in *The New York Times* or *The Wall Street Journal*. You got it if you heard about it from someone like my Uncle Louie who worked in a "speakeasy," "protected" by the Mob. Louie spoke to the speakeasy's owner, who spoke to Rose, who owned the candy store in front of the newsstand. Rebecca's modest English-language skills were not an obstacle: the less Rebecca knew about the candy store and who frequented it, the better. Rose liked Rebecca so she called the Shapiros, who called the Mob, who agreed. The Lieberman family borrowed the money from a commercial bank, and Rebecca became a "capitalist."

III. All the News That's Fit to Sell

Rebecca lived a mile from the newsstand. Every weekday, my Uncle Al, Aunt Mildred's husband, Rebecca's brother-in-law, dropped Rebecca off on his way to work. Every night, he picked her up. Rebecca never had to walk. Rebecca worked five days a week and half a day on Sundays. On Sundays, in the summer, she started at 7:00 a.m., and caught the families going to the beach or ballgame. In the winter, she caught the same families going to Manhattan to the museums and the planetarium. She did not work on Saturdays — she was, to the best of her ability, an observant Jew.

On weekdays, Rebecca opened the newsstand from 6:00 a.m. to 11:00 a.m. to get the morning commuters and from 3:00 p.m. to 9:00 p.m. to catch the evening commuters, From 11:00 a.m. to 3:00 p.m. she rested in Rose's — they had become good friends, unlike the previous lease holder. Rebecca sold newspapers: the *Times*, the *Herald*, the *Tribune*, the *Journal*, the *American*, the *Post*, and *PM*. She sold the Communist Party's *Daily Worker*, and the Yiddish *Der Tog* and *Forverts*. She sold magazines: *Time*, *Newsweek*, *Life*, *Look*, *The Saturday Evening Post*, *Collier's*, *Popular Science*, and *Popular Mechanics*. If she did not have a particular newspaper or magazine, she could get it by the time the customer came home from work.

She sold cigarettes, in packs and cartons, cigars singly and in boxes, pipes and pipe tobacco. Everyone smoked, but not

Rebecca. She tried it, disliked it, and quit. She sold candy bars: Hershey, Nestle, Baby Ruth, and Oh Henry!. She sold combs, hairbrushes, lipstick, and toothpaste for commuters who were in a hurry and "fixed" their faces on the train or in the office.

Every day, Abe Reles's cousin brought canisters of coffee, dozens of bagels, sandwiches, and knishes: puffed pastries filled with meat or potatoes. How Rebecca, standing on her feet, rarely moving, managed to pour coffee, slice bagels, sell toiletries, and laugh, joke, and not lose her temper was a marvel. If Joe DiMaggio, the great Yankee center fielder of the 1930s and 1940s was "Grace-in-Motion," Rebecca was "Grace-in-Position." There were things she did not do: she did not date her customers, she did not sell liquor (a speakeasy offered to supply her), and she did not sell "French postcards" of naughty ladies in naughty positions. Abe Reles's cousin, Manny, offered to supply her. He also propositioned her. She refused — unequivocally.

Initially, Rebecca wondered how Rose made a living. Rose had given up all the moneymaking concessions: newspapers, magazines, cigarettes, candy bars, bagels, and coffee. There were only a few things you could get at Rose's you could not get at Rebecca's. Rose had a refrigerator, Rebecca did not. You could get an ice-cream soda at Rose's but not at Rebecca's. Rose sold, at most, five ice-cream sodas a day. Rose made 25 cents on each soda: could you pay the rent on $1.25 a day? The secret was that Rose's candy store was a front: in the back of Rose's, behind a secret door, was a gambling parlor, one that later, under Abe Reles, rivaled modern-day Las Vegas. There were slot machines, Poker and 21, tables, radios tuned to the latest baseball games, boxing matches, and horseracing tracks. There were bookmakers ready to give you "odds" and loan sharks ready to lend you money. The Mob got a cut, the police got a cut, and Rose got a cut. That is why she did not care if she sold a single ice-cream soda. That is why she only wanted customers who were gamblers in her store. And that is why she stayed open 20 hours a day. When, after a few days, Rebecca figured this out, she and Rose, without saying a word, agreed to know as little as possible about each other's business. The previous leaseholder, the one without a brain stem or cerebellum, could not figure this out — he wanted a cut.

IV. A Wasserman Test's for Swollen Feet

In 1929, Rebecca, having worked at the newsstand for nine years, noticed her legs, below her knees, and her feet were swollen. In the past, they had swelled during the day but subsided at night — after lying down. She asked her family. No one knew. She asked her pharmacists, the Plotkin brothers, who served as surrogate physicians. They looked at her calves, asked if the swelling subsided at night, and when told it did not referred her to Dr. Wasserman.

There were three Drs. Wassermans: Seth, the father, whose parents arrived in America in 1870. Seth graduated from the New York University Medical School and established a general practice in Brownsville. He bought a house on Saratoga Avenue half a block from Pitkin, and a quarter of a mile from the place that would be Rose's candy store and Rebecca's newsstand. The ground floor had the waiting and exam rooms and a

Brontez Purnell, still from *Free Jazz*, 2013, 8 mm film. Performed by Brontez Purnell Dance Company.

lead-shielded X-ray suite. The upper floor housed the family quarters. There were stained-glass windows, two elms, and an oak tree in front and a small vegetable garden in back.

Sheldon and Sam also graduated from the NYU Medical School and joined their father in practice. The Wassermans were Polish Jews unrelated to Professor August von Wassermann, a German count, who in 1908 developed the Wassermann test, one that told you if you had ever been infected with syphilis. Before penicillin, syphilis was a killer, and to "contain" it anyone getting married had to go for a Wassermann.

In 1918, Seth Wasserman while attending his patients got the Flu and died. Seth passed it to his sons, who survived, and to his wife, who died.

Sheldon, the older Wasserman son, was born in 1896. He was five feet, eight inches tall, captain of his college baseball team, and a member of the medical honor society. He was his parents' favorite. He was an astute diagnostician with a calming, reassuring manner whether or not this was warranted. If you did not want to know how seriously ill you were, Sheldon was your doctor. And popular he was.

Sam, the younger Wasserman son, was born in 1900. He was five feet, six inches tall, stocky, and non-athletic. He was as astute as Sheldon but suffered under his brother's shadow. He had a dreadful bedside manner — he told the truth. If you left their office and had been seen by Dr. Sam and diagnosed with what was in the early 20th century a fatal and largely untreatable disease such as syphilis, or tuberculosis, or endocarditis, or encephalitis, you left in tears. If, however, with the same illness you saw Dr. Sheldon, you left cheerful because he was going to beat whatever it was you had. If you had seen Sam and you wanted to see Sheldon, you could if you came on a Tuesday when Sam was away, working in a radiologist's office in Manhattan. You did not want to hurt Dr. Sam's feelings because some day, in an emergency, you might need him. Some especially unhappy patients compared Dr. Sam, to one of the dwarfs in *Snow White*, in the late 1930s a popular movie. Most said "Bashful," none said "Dopey."

Dr. Sam looked at Rebecca's legs. He had her lie down and noted the swelling did not go away. He raised one of her legs and held it up 90 degrees at the hip. The swelling did not go down. He then, with his finger, indented her thigh. The thigh remained indented for several minutes after he removed his finger. "You have got terribly swollen legs, from you ankles to your ass," he said. "Do you stand on them?" he asked.

"Twelve hours a day," she replied. "I own a newsstand."

"You walk?" he asked.

"No," she replied.

"You should," he said. Next, he commented, "Your fat, that contributes to the swelling. Lose weight!"

"How?" she asked. "I am surrounded all day by candy bars, bagels, and knishes."

"Try," he replied. "Do you salt your food?"

"Yes," she replied.

"Don't," he rejoined.

He then inspected the many twisting, turning, blue-colored, corkscrew-shaped veins running from her ankles to her knees: varicose veins. Next, he took her took her blood pressure in both arms, checking for a narrowed artery in one or both arms. Her blood pressures were normal. He asked if she had anything wrong with her heart, lungs, kidneys, or liver. When she answered, "No," he asked if there was any family history of disease. "Only poverty," she replied.

He then listened to her heart and lungs, felt her liver, and felt all the pulses in her legs. Holding up a large drawing of the heart, lungs, arteries, and veins, he explained, "The heart is a pump, it propels oxygen rich blood through the arteries into the capillaries. This forward pressure on the capillaries is opposed by a back pressure from the veins. If the pump fails and arterial pressure drops, the legs will swell. This is not the cause in you."

"Blood is 'pushed up' the veins toward the heart by the action of the muscles of your legs that act as tiny 'motors.' Blood is prevented from flowing back toward the capillaries and arteries by one-way valves strategically placed along the vein. It is thought a defect in the valve leads to pooling of blood in the vein stretching and twisting it. Once the vein enlarges and once enough veins enlarge, the legs begin to swell. You can have swelling without varicose veins and varicose veins without swelling, but if you have varicose veins and swelling the varicose veins came first. Does your mother have varicose veins?"

"Yes," she replied.

"What does she do?" he asked.

"She sits all day and rocks," she replied.

"Perhaps," he said, "the defect in you and your mother's veins is genetic. Then again, your mother, unlike you, does not stand on her feet all day. And your mother, unlike you, has had six children: this can promote the emergence of varicose veins. If you stand too long, and you do, venous pressure increases, and your legs swell. If you exercise the muscles in your legs will act as 'motors' forcing blood back to your heart. Do you ride a bicycle?"

"I did," she said. "Then I fell twice and was hit by a car once. Do you want it? It's only dented in back?"

"No," he replied. Then he asked, "Do you wear elastic stockings? They straighten and support the veins."

"I live alone," she replied, "in the morning I cannot get them on, at night I cannot get them off."

"Get help," he replied. "Get a boyfriend."

"Are you available?" she asked mischievously.

"No!" he replied. Then he asked, "Have you tried a diuretic?"

"A water pill?" she answered. "Once, after work, my brother-in law took me to a doctor who injected me with a diuretic. An hour later, I wet my pants. All night I could not sleep because I kept going to the bathroom. In the morning, when my brother-in-law came to take me to work, I collapsed. In the emergency room, they said I had low 'salts,' sodium, and potassium. They kept me two days. Later, I learned the diuretic had mercury, and mercury is used to treat syphilis."

"The amount of mercury in the diuretic is much lower than the dose used to treat syphilis," he replied. "I don't think you were harmed by the mercury."

"You were not injected with the diuretic, you did not wet your bed," she said. "And you did not pass out in the emergency room. The doctor nearly killed me."

V. Varicose Veins, the Stock Market, and Adolf Hitler

"Varicose veins are unsightly but rarely fatal," said Dr. Sam. "There is a surgical treatment for them called stripping and ligation. But I would not recommend it."

"You said, 'Varicose veins are rarely fatal.' How do you die from a varicose vein?" asked Rebecca.

"You form a blood clot in one of them," replied Dr. Sam, "the clot travels to your heart, then to your lungs, destroys part of your lungs, and you die."

"Thanks for the information," said Rebecca, "I will think about it."

"Look, you are a nice lady but the chemistry between us does not seem good. Go see my brother, Dr. Sheldon — I will not be insulted."

"I will," Rebecca said.

In October 1929, the Stock Market crashed, and America entered the Great Depression. No one had money for food, much less doctors and medicines. From 1929 to 1933, business on Wall Street, the Garment Center, and Rebecca's newsstand was less than half of what it had been. Rebecca survived because she was single, lived with her mother, and ate part of her business: the bagels, candy bars, and knishes. As the economy shrank and Rebecca stood longer, her calves swelled more. Her calves and the Dow Jones Industrial Average (DJIA) were locked in a deadly spiral: as the DJIA fell, the swelling of her legs rose.

In 1934, under Franklin D. Roosevelt the economy began to recover. In New York, a new District Attorney, Thomas E. Dewey, turned Murder, Inc. and the Mob upside down. Several mobsters, including the chief, Lucky Luciano, were exiled back to Italy. The Mob's financial guru, Meyer Lansky, left for Florida. Abe Reles, to save his life from the electric chair, turned informer. He then lost his life to the Mob — being pushed out of an 11th-story building without a parachute, umbrella, or wings. Rose kept her candy store and her innocence, claiming she had no idea gambling was taking place in her back room.

In 1936, as Adolf Hitler marched into the Rhineland, in the first step toward World War II, Marge Shapiro, no relation to any of the dead Shapiro brothers, a nurse at the Manhattan clinic where Sheldon worked, marched into Sheldon's life, and stayed. They were married, and Marge joined Sheldon in Brownsville. In 1938, Rebecca's father died suddenly — either of a heart attack or a pulmonary embolism. There was no autopsy. Sheldon assured Rebecca that a heart attack was a more likely diagnosis. Rebecca was *not* reassured. She kept looking at her legs and her enlarged tortuous veins.

Rebecca moved back with her mother. Her mother, my grandmother, had diabetes. Each day my grandfather had checked my grandmother's urine with a "dipstick," indicating how much sugar there was in the urine and how much insulin he should inject. My grandmother could not do this because she was blind. Dr. Sam, my grandmother's doctor, explained this to Rebecca who was now in "charge" of my grandmother's diabetes.

Dr. Sam explained that urinary sugar represented an "average" of blood sugar over 12 to 24 hours. To properly regulate blood sugar, he had to know her fasting sugar. Several times a month Rebecca took my grandmother to a lab where a technician drew her blood. She did not have "good veins" — they were hard to find and bled easily. Half the time they had to call Dr. Sam or Dr. Sheldon, who would have my grandmother lie down and jab a needle "blindly" into her femoral vein. The femoral vein lies near the femoral artery. Dr. Sheldon could, and once did, hit the artery, which spurted blood like an oil well until it was "capped" by applying pressure for almost an hour. My grandmother, Rebecca, Drs. Sam and Sheldon, and the lab dreaded the blood drawing.

In 1940, Hitler occupied Holland, Belgium, and France and threatened England. Roosevelt, fearing America was next on Hitler's "menu," called for and Congress approved a first-ever peacetime draft. War, if it came would be global. The Army would need lightweight uniforms for fighting in the deserts of Africa and the jungles of the Southwest Pacific, heavy woolen uniforms, and overcoats for the mountains of Italy and the forests of France. The Army Air Corps would need heavy leather jackets for the interiors of their non-pressurized bombers and fighters. The Marines, the Navy, the Coast Guard, and our Allies would have their own special needs.

The Garment District and Brownsville were never so busy. My father made more overcoats in a year than in his previous 10. Rebecca, to keep up, hired two ladies to assist her. Rose reopened her back parlor, the same Mob, in nicer suits, returned and gambling resumed. The police did not care, they had more important things to do like catching spies.

In 1940, Rebecca's mother died suddenly. It could have been a heart attack; it could have been an embolism — from a varicose vein. (The anticoagulant properties of aspirin and warfarin were unknown in 1940.)

Rebecca's legs had become heavier, colder, more painful. Her feet were mottled, purplish-blue, resembling a cadaver's. To walk, she wore men's shoes. They were wider, more comfortable, and sturdier. She gave up style for safety. The great saphenous vein, the main superficial vein of each leg, the one emptying into the deep femoral vein, the vein where clots form, had grown from a trickle to a "raging river." Rebecca worried she would die of an embolism.

VI. Roosevelt, the Draft, Rebecca's Legs

Roosevelt's draft included doctors. Sheldon, because he was married, was excluded; Sam was not. He was assigned to the Army's induction center in Lower Manhattan and did physical examinations on potential recruits. It was not stimulating or exciting, but it allowed him a day off every two weeks to visit Rebecca. On Sunday, November 30, 1941, on a day when, for New York, it was exceptionally warm, they sat in the backyard of Sam's home and talked.

Two weeks ago, Sheldon had not recommended but urged her to see a surgeon about her legs. She had agreed. Sheldon recommended his and Sam's professor at the NYU Medical Center, Dr. Phil Smith, a "legend" in the emerging field of vascular surgery. At 60, he was nearing the end of his career. A memorable teacher, a master surgeon, he was known internationally, and had operated on some of the best-known personalities of the 1930s and 1940s. He was to surgery what Babe Ruth was to baseball, what Jack Dempsey was to boxing, what FDR was to politics.

Rebecca had seen Dr. Smith in his offices at the Graduate Hospital on 20th Street and Second Avenue in Manhattan. The Graduate Hospital was the private hospital of the NYU Medical Center. It was replaced in 1963 by the Tisch Hospital and later by the Kimmel Pavilion. Dr. Smith recommended surgery and scheduled it for Tuesday, December 2, 1941.

"Why," asked Sam, "was I kept out of the loop?"

Brontez Purnell, *Unstoppable Feat: The Dances of Ed Mock*, 2018. Image courtesy of the artist and DIS.

I have been filming a documentary on the life of Ed Mock, a Black, queer experimental choreographer.

I have often sat looking at pictures of the man, going over and over in my head what his fears, frustrations, and anxieties were. There must have been many. His position as a gay Black man in the classically White world of modern dance proved difficult — sometimes calling into question his legitimacy. Mock was not just a jazz dancer, as the world wanted to neatly categorize him. His work combined elements of performance, pedestrian movement, and acting technique, all meeting in the singularity that was Mock himself a prolific postmodernist well before that identity was accessible. He paid a price for this, of course, which many in his circle believe to be the reason that much of his practice (compared to his contemporaries') went underfunded.

As queer people, art makers, radicals, and allies alike, many of us are still deep in the process of excavating the memories of our fallen spiritual family, in every sense of the word. We are often surprised to find the bits and pieces of their lives peeking through buried histories.

As a queer Black dancer and choreographer in the Bay Area, it is humbling for me to know that I am not the first or the last, but part of a tradition. I am not here to invent the wheel but to take on the equally taxing challenge of keeping it moving forward and sometimes torturing myself with this question: "What would the world look like if he had lived?" – Brontez Purnell

"Because you would have exaggerated the risks, downplayed the benefits, and created so much doubt I would have cancelled the operation. We met because of my legs, we spend our time talking about my legs, you are afraid if my legs are 'cured' we will drift apart," replied Rebecca.

"You have been reading too much Freud," said Sam, "he's a fraud."

"Perhaps," replied Rebecca, "but I think in some things he is correct, the hidden reason for doing something is often the real reason. You are not interested in my legs; you are interested in what is between them. But are afraid to say so."

"Too much Freud!" yelled Sam. "I have rearranged my schedule so I can be with you. Do not argue because it is done."

On the morning of December 1, Rebecca and Sam arrived at the Graduate Hospital in a chauffeur-driven car. They had not spoken until they checked in and were directed to the hematology and chemistry lab. When the technician approached with a large-bore needle and syringe, Rebecca nearly fainted and was placed on a stretcher. "She has brittle veins," Sam said, "you will get no blood. She has a good vein on the inside aspect of her left arm but they are saving that as an emergency line for the surgery."

Then, before he could be stopped, Sam grabbed the needle and syringe, picked up Rebecca's skirt, exposed her groin, and expertly plunged the needle into her right femoral vein. In 2021, he would have been arrested; in 1941, a doctor was god. After her blood was drawn, after her urine was collected, she was wheeled into a small room where she underwent a physical examination by a junior resident. Next a technician did an electrocardiogram (ECG). She showed it to the resident, who said it was normal, and he showed it to Sam, who agreed. After the technician left, an aide wheeled her to X-ray where she had films of her chest and abdomen. A radiologist, a classmate of Sam's, read the X-rays and pronounced them normal. He was introduced to Rebecca and commented on how good a doctor Sam was.

Rebecca had "graduated" from a stretcher to a wheelchair with Sam pushing her. It was lunchtime, and Sam took her to the doctors' dining room where a veritable parade of doctors greeted him. Some were classmates, some were surgeons to whom he referred patients, and some were doctors he knew from the Academy of Medicine, the New York Society of Medicine. And the New York Medical Licensing Board. Rebecca was impressed, she had never been part of this aspect of Sam's life, had not known how highly regarded he was. Some of the doctors assumed Rebecca was Sam's girlfriend and in a good-natured way said she had better grab him before someone else did.

In the late afternoon, Sam wheeled Rebecca into a large room where a technician with a Kodak camera took colored pictures of her legs: anterior-posterior, lateral-medial. To Dr. Smith, it was merely a logical way of following his patients. To others in the field, it was revolutionary. After all the pictures had been taken, Sam wheeled Rebecca to her room. "Sam," she said, "I am sorry I acted like a bitch. I was scared. I could not have gotten through this without you."

"I could not have gotten through the day not knowing what was happening to you," replied Sam.

"About my legs," she said, "and what's between them, when this is over, I'll say what Mae West says, 'Come up and see me sometime.'"

"Is that an invitation?" he asked.

"Yes," she replied.

VII. A Medical Mistake

After Sam left and Rebecca was helped into bed, two residents came by. The senior looked at her chart and said, "No one drew blood for a potassium. Draw it Stat!"

The junior remarked, "She's got no veins."

"Just get the blood," said the senior.

For the next hour, the junior, the senior, and the chief resident tried and failed to get blood from Rebecca. Finally they found a vein on the outer surface of her left "pinky," gave the chief a tiny bore needle, and he plunged it in, piercing the vein, causing it to bleed. Next, he drew out the blood, and gave it to the junior resident to run to the lab. Rebecca stood up and started to leave. It required three aides to hold her down.

An hour later, the lab called and reported a serum potassium of 6.8 millimoles/liter. Normal is 3.5 to 5.5 mmol/L. A level of 6.8 mmol/L is lethal. Potassium is the main intracellular cation, a high serum level means cells in the heart, muscles, and kidneys are "leaking" potassium, and if the leak is not stopped the body will shut down.

In 1941, the main treatment for a high serum potassium was intravenous insulin, which drives potassium back into the cells. To counteract the potential for a dangerously low sugar from IV insulin, glucose is administered IV. Where the residents found two open veins, one for insulin and one for glucose, where they found a large open vein to monitor the serum levels of glucose and potassium, will never be known. Some say the residents

had better eyes than anyone else, some say they drew the blood from Rebecca's varicose veins. By 7:00 a.m., the situation had "stabilized." The IV glucose had caused Rebecca to pee through half a dozen bed sheets. What was not soaked in urine was soaked in blood.

At 7:00 a.m., Dr. Smith, Dr. Sheldon Wasserman, and Dr. Sam Wasserman appeared. They surveyed the scene, which resembled a Bruegel painting, Bedlam, London during the Blitz. While Sam ran to free Rebecca, who had screamed for help when she saw him, Dr. Smith coolly and calmly took a report from each of the residents, the nurses, the aides, and the lab technician. He examined Rebecca. She was suffering, temporarily, from the medical equivalent of "shell shock" and should recover. He then "invited" the residents and the Wassermans into a small room. He turned to the chief resident and asked, "What is the most common cause of hyperkalemia, high potassium?"

The chief resident replied. "Drawing blood from a traumatized vein, it causes potassium to be released from the walls of the vein."

"So," said Dr. Smith, "does this mean potassium is elevated throughout the blood or is it only elevated locally?"

"It is only elevated locally," said the chief resident.

"If I traumatized a vein in the right arm and drew blood from that vein and had a high potassium, then I cleanly and atraumatically drew blood from a vein in the left arm, would I expect a high or a normal serum potassium?"

"You would expect a normal potassium," said the chief resident.

"When you found a 'lethal' level of potassium, did you draw blood from another more distant vein?" asked Dr. Smith.

"No," replied the chief.

"In short," said Dr. Smith, "this was a falsely high serum potassium, and you mistook it for a truly high serum potassium, panicked, and began a potentially 'lethal treatment' with insulin and glucose."

"Yes," replied the chief.

Turning to the senior resident, Dr. Smith asked, "What are the physical signs of a high potassium?"

"Muscle weakness," replied the senior.

"This lady," said Dr. Smith, "when I arrived was held down by three aides. How weak could she be?"

"Not weak at all," replied the senior.

"What is another sign of hyperkalemia?" asked Dr. Smith.

"Anuria, lack of urine," replied the senior.

"This lady pissed through six layers of bedsheets, so I presume her kidneys are working," said Dr. Smith. "Give me another sign of hyperkalemia." "Shortness of breath," said the senior.

"This lady was screaming so loud you could hear her when you entered the building. Is this a sign of shortness of breath?" asked Dr. Smith. "No, of course not." Turning to the junior resident he asked, "What did the ECG show?"

"I read it with the cardiologist," said the junior. "It was normal."

"Have you ever heard of hyperkalemia with a normal cardiogram?" asked Dr. Smith. "Has anyone in this world heard of hyperkalemia with a normal cardiogram? Do not bother looking it up, the answer is *no*."

"Look boys, you messed up, you could have killed the lady. You should not have panicked, should have looked at the lady, looked at the ECG, looked at the potassium, seen there was a mismatch, and asked what does not fit — the potassium does not fit."

"I am not going to punish you," continued Dr. Smith. "I am certain you will remember this. It is December 2, 1941, my sources tell me before the year is out, we will be at war with Japan and possibly Germany and Italy. We will need you boys in the field. Apologize to the lady and learn from it."

Rebecca composed herself, listened to the apologies, judged them to be sincere, and accepted them. She then joined Dr. Smith, Sam, and Sheldon. "What do you want to do about the surgery?" asked Dr. Smith.

"The indications for surgery before the 'mistake' have not changed. The 'mistake' did not occur *at* surgery, it occurred in a lab, it could have occurred in my office or Sam's office. I say go," said Sheldon.

"I wanted the surgery before the 'mishap,'" said Rebecca, "and the 'mishap' hasn't changed my mind. I am tired of my legs always hurting, I am tired of their always being cold, and I am tired of wearing men's shoes."

"I was against the surgery before the 'mishap,' afraid she would die *at* surgery," said Sam. "Looking at what happened, she's safer in Dr. Smith's OR than in crossing Saratoga Avenue."

The operation was a success, Sam and Rebecca married, Rebecca sold the newsstand, and the three surgical residents joined the Navy the day after Pearl Harbor.

Brontez Purnell, *Unstoppable Feat: The Dances of Ed Mock*, 2018. Image courtesy of the artist and DIS.

Kristen Brownell is a writer and educator living in Los Angeles. After escaping and recovering from domestic violence, substance abuse issues, and life on the streets, she went on to earn her MFA in Creative Nonfiction from the University of California at Riverside and is currently pursuing her PhD in English at the Claremont Colleges, where she specializes in teaching second-language learners. She recently completed a memoir, *Lost Vegas*, about her wild ride from high school dropout to dishwasher to dancer to down-and-out to doctor. Kristen is also in the process of launching a non-for-profit, Home for Education, which aims to help homeless, almost homeless, and formerly homeless women start and complete their educational journey. She can be found at www.kristenbrownell.com.

Michelle Cho is assistant professor of East Asian Popular Cultures and Cinema Studies at the University of Toronto. She's published on Asian cinemas and Korean wave television, video, and pop music in such venues as *Cinema Journal*, *The Korean Popular Culture Reader*, *Asian Video Cultures*, and *Rediscovering Korean Cinema*. Her writing can also be found online at evenmagazine.com, flowjournal.org, and pandemicmedia.meson.press.

Raphael Cormack is a writer and translator. He has edited two collections of short stories translated from Arabic, *The Book of Cairo* and *The Book of Khartoum* (with Max Shmookler). His first book, *Midnight in Cairo*, was published in 2021. He has a PhD in Egyptian Theatre from the University of Edinburgh.

Louisa Hall is an assistant professor of Creative Writing at the University of Iowa. Her novels include *Speak* (Ecco, 2015) and *Trinity* (Ecco, 2018).

Langdon Hammer is the Niel Gray Jr. Professor of English at Yale. He is the author of *Hames Merrill: Life and Art* and, with Stephen Yenser, co-editor of *A Whole World: Letters from James Merrill*. He is working on a critical biography of Elizabeth Bishop.

Edward Hirsch has published 10 books of poems, including *Gabriel: A Poem* and *Stranger by Night*, and six books of prose, most newly *100 Poems to Break Your Heart*.

Nancy Kricorian is the author of the novels *Zabelle*, *Dreams of Bread and Fire*, and *All the Light There Was*, which are focused on post-Genocide Armenian diaspora life. Her essays and poems have appeared in *Guernica*, *Parnassus*, *Minnesota Review*, *The Mississippi Review*, *Witness*, and other journals. She is currently at work on a novel about Armenians in Beirut during the Lebanese Civil War.

Lavinia Liang's writings have appeared in *The Guardian*, *TIME*, *Catapult*, *VICE*, and elsewhere.

Abraham Lieberman is a neurologist. He was born in Brooklyn in 1938, graduated from Cornell University with a degree in history in 1959, and completed his stories at the New York University School of Medicine in 1963. He was a professor of neurology at the New York University Medical Center from 1970 to 1989, at the

Barrow Neurological Institute in Phoenix, Arizona from 1989 to 1999, and at the University of Miami from 1999 to 2007, and was the Lonnie and Muhammad Ali Professor of Neurology at Barrow from 2007 to 2018. Lieberman has authored or co-authored 200 peer reviewed papers, mainly on Parkinson's disease, brain tumors, and stroke and five popular books for patients with Parkinson's. He was Muhammad Ali's doctor for 30 years and is recognized as a world authority on Adolf Hitler's Parkinson's and Franklin D. Roosevelt's polio.

Stephen Marche is a writer from Toronto. His next book, *The Next Civil War*, will be released in January 2022.

Sarah McEachern is a reader and writer in Brooklyn, New York. Some of her recent writing has been published by *The Ploughshares Blog, BOMB, The Believer, The Rumpus, Split Lip Mag*, and *Full Stop*. Personal essays and fiction have been published by *Entropy, Catapult, Pacifica Literary Review*, and *Pigeon Pages* among others.

Natasha Rao is the author of *Latitude*, which won the APR/Honickman First Book Prize and is forthcoming in September 2021. Her work appears or will soon appear in *The American Poetry Review, The Yale Review, Poetry Northwest, Narrative*, and elsewhere. She lives in Brooklyn.

Natalia Reyes is from Indio, California. Her writing has appeared in *Nexos* and *Fifth Wednesday Journal*. She is an alumna of the Iowa Writers' Workshop, where she was a Paul & Daisy Soros Fellow, a Provost's Visiting Writer Fellow in

Fiction, and the recipient of the Taylor-Chehak Prize.

Prageeta Sharma's recent poetry collection is *Grief Sequence*, out from Wave Books. She is the founder of the conference Thinking Its Presence, an interdisciplinary conference on race, creative writing, and artistic and aesthetic practices. A recipient of the 2010 Howard Foundation Award and a finalist for the 2020 Four Quartets Prize, she taught at the University of Montana and now teaches at Pomona College.

Dujie Tahat is a Filipino-Jordanian immigrant living in Washington State. They are the author of *Here I Am O My God*, selected for a Poetry Society of America Chapbook Fellowship, and *Salat*, selected as winner of the Tupelo Press Sunken Garden Chapbook Award and longlisted for the 2020 PEN/Voelcker Award for Poetry Collection. Along with Luther Hughes and Gabrielle Bates, they co-host *The Poet Salon* podcast.

Michael Torres was born and brought up in Pomona, California, where he spent his adolescence as a graffiti artist. His debut collection of poems, *An Incomplete List of Names* (Beacon Press, 2020), was selected by Raquel Salas Rivera for the National Poetry Series and named one of *NPR*'s Best Books of 2020. Currently, he's an assistant professor in the MFA program at Minnesota State University, Mankato, and a teaching artist with the Minnesota Prison Writing Workshop. He can be found at www.michaeltorreswriter.com.

Leah Umansky is the author of two full-length collections: *The Barbarous Century* and *Domestic Uncertainties*. She earned her MFA in Poetry at Sarah Lawrence College and is the curator and host of The COUPLET Reading Series in NYC. Her poems have appeared or are forthcoming in such places as *Thrush Poetry Journal*, *Glass Poetry Journal*, *The New York Times*, *POETRY*, *Guernica*, *The Bennington Review*, The Academy of American Poets' *Poem-A-Day*, *Rhino*, and *Pleiades*. She can be found at www.leahumansky.com.

FEATURED ARTISTS

Mona Varichon is an artist and translator living in Paris, currently in residence at the Cité Internationale des Arts. Recent exhibitions and screenings of her work include the Jeu de Paume Lab (Paris, France), the ICA London (London, UK), Mascot (Los Angeles, CA), The Renaissance Society (Chicago, IL), u's (Diamond Valley, Canada), CAPC musée d'art contemporain (Bordeaux, France), High Art (Paris, France), L'Etna (Montreuil, FR), Redcat (Los Angeles, CA), The Echo Park Film Center (Los Angeles, CA) and The Egyptian Theatre (Hollywood, CA). She is currently translating the memoirs of American underground filmmakers George and Mike Kuchar into French, to be published by her imprint Varichon & Cie.

Brontez Purnell is a writer, musician, dancer, filmmaker, and performance artist. He is the author of a graphic novel, a novella, a children's book, and the novel *Since I Laid My Burden Down*. Recipient of a 2018 Whiting Award for Fiction, he was named one of the 32 Black Male Writers for Our Time by *T: New York Times Style Magazine* in 2018.

Purnell is also the frontman for the band the Younger Lovers, the co-founder of the experimental dance group the Brontez Purnell Dance Company, the creator of the renowned cult zine *Fag School*, and the director of several short films, music videos, and, most recently, the documentary *Unstoppable Feat: Dances of Ed Mock*. He recently released his current novel "100 Boyfriends" on FSGxMCD. Born in Triana, Alabama, he's lived in Oakland, California, for 19 years.

Kayla Ephros (b. 1992, New Jersey) is an artist, poet and educator living in Los Angeles.

Ed Mock was an avant-garde San Francisco-based dancer and choreographer known for his mixture of classical dance with experimentally-inclined and improvisatory performance art. He ran the West Coast Dance Company (1974-1979) and Ed Mock Dancers (1980-1985). He died from an AIDS-related illness in 1986.

Narumi Nekpenekpen (b. 1998, Kashiwa, Japan) is an artist based in Long Beach, California. Recent exhibitions include *Center of the Core* at Deli Gallery (New York, NY) and *Made in L.A. 2020: a version* via *VIVID* at the Hammer Museum (Los Angeles, CA). She has forthcoming exhibitions at Soft Opening (London, UK) and Real Pain (New York, NY).